THE ART OF THE TRUMPET-MAKER

EARLY MUSIC SERIES

THE ART OF THE TRUMPET-MAKER

The Materials, Tools, and Techniques
of the Seventeenth and Eighteenth Centuries
in Nuremberg

ROBERT BARCLAY

CLARENDON PRESS · OXFORD

Oxford University Press, Walton Street, Oxford OX2 6DP
Oxford New York
Athens Auckland Bangkok Bombay
Calcutta Cape Town Dar es Salaam Delhi
Florence Hong Kong Istanbul Karachi
Kuala Lumpur Madras Madrid Melbourne
Mexico City Nairobi Paris Singapore
Taipei Tokyo Toronto
and associated companies in
Berlin Ibadan

Oxford is a trade mark of Oxford University Press

Published in the United States
by Oxford University Press, New York

British Library Cataloguing in Publication Data
Data available

Library of Congress Cataloging in Publication Data
Data available
ISBN 0–19–816605–2

Printed in Great Britain
on acid-free paper by
St. Edmundsbury Press,
Bury St. Edmunds, Suffolk

PREFACE

This is not a do-it-yourself manual on how to make a classic Nuremberg trumpet, although a competent metal-worker with experience in the processes described in Chapter 6 would have no difficulty in producing an instrument far superior to many offered for sale today. In spite of the title, there is more to this book than just the art of the trumpet-maker. During a review of other chapters, I was asked why I had dwelt so long on such matters as the sources and production of raw materials, the nature of metals, the location and history of Nuremberg, and even safety in the workshop. I think the answer is simply that I want this to be as general a description of all the processes from the raw material to the finished object as possible. No artefact exists in isolation from those who made it. In contrast to the philosophy of the *Kunstkammer*, where only the rarest and most beautiful objects are isolated from their milieu, the vast majority of musical instruments are implements which were made by ordinary people and used by them. I would like the reader to have a very wide idea of the range of processes, materials, techniques and tools which needed to be focused upon the finished object, and of the huge, anonymous army of labourers which supported all craftsmen. Too often descriptions of artefacts (instruments in particular) miss the human angle expressed in the interlocking social machine which produced such utensils, concentrating rather on the great solo craftsman working in splendid isolation. I know of no such creature.

With our modern easy access to materials and finished work, we are inclined to forget what happens 'behind the scenes'. I would like metal-workers, brass players, scholars, and students to know on a practical, material level what the early trumpet actually is—for their own information and intellectual pleasure, but also so that in the future the natural trumpet might enjoy the real revival it has deserved for so long. This book cannot help but give that revival a small push in the right direction.

This book would, of course, have been impossible without the assistance of many colleagues and friends. I would like to thank in particular Edward H. Tarr for his enthusiasm from the first idea to the finished manuscript, and Don L. Smithers for his wise counsel. Production of the manuscript relied very heavily on the resources of the Canadian Conservation Institute, Department of Communications, and special thanks should go to Maureen Clarke of the CCI Library for the many requests for research material which she handled. Individual chapters were reviewed by a number of colleagues. I am particularly grateful to Martha Goodway, Karl Hachenberg, and Lyndsie Selwyn for their help with my inadequate understanding of metal, Philip R. White, David Edwards, Gary Stewart, Henry Fischer, and Graham Nicholson for review of tools and techniques, and Robert Oades, Thomas Strang,

Jeremy Montagu, and David Tremain for their general overview. Friedemann Hellwig started me thinking along these lines some years ago when he first suggested I write an article on the topic, while Timothy J. McGee threw me into the furnace when he asked me to teach a course on brass instrument making techniques. Peter Vogel very kindly assisted me with the more difficult translations. Carl Bigras and Jeremy Powell advised me on photography, while my daughter Anne pressed the shutter on numerous occasions. Many other individuals helped in a number of ways and I take this opportunity to thank them all. Finally, the tolerance and understanding of my family has by now been well tested. It remains to be seen how much more they will let me get away with.

R.B.

CONTENTS

LIST OF FIGURES

List of Figures

I

Introduction

It should be emphasised that . . . no special instrument was used by the old players, nor did they carry to their graves any lost secret which has never since been
recovered. The sounds of the 4th octave, and even higher, are still there, and
could be elicited by any player endowed with the right natural gifts . . .

Adam Carse

Prologue

In order to explore and express to the maximum the music of any period, the musician must make himself at home in the composer's workshop. He must be well
aware of what tools the composer had at his disposal; what he could and could not
do. It is the obligation of the musician to make every effort to hear and understand
the music as the composer did. Of particular importance, the musician must be at
home with the virtues and limitations of the contemporary instruments. An adequate realization of the composer's intentions can only be approached when thorough attention is given to authenticity in instrumentation and technique. This is
especially so in the case of early music for the trumpet, whose true renaissance still
lies in the future. The modern trumpet and its pre-industrial forebear, the natural
trumpet, vary so widely mechanically and acoustically, and require playing techniques at such wide variance, that they might almost be regarded as different instruments. Performance of trumpet music of the seventeenth and eighteenth
centuries has posed problems for players trained on the valved trumpets of the
modern orchestra, resulting in the use of compromise instruments, perhaps the
most popular of which are the 'natural' trumpet equipped with anti-nodal finger
holes, and the piccolo valve trumpet.[1]

This book is about trumpet-*making*. It is not the intention to dwell upon the various arguments concerning authenticity and practicality; there is no intention of discussing the merits of playing uncompromised natural trumpets (this has been done
elsewhere by scholars and players more qualified than this author) except to say that

---

[1] It would be informative if the term 'natural trumpet' were better defined in record liner notes; most of the so-
called natural trumpets heard on recordings are, in fact, quite un-natural.

it is entirely pointless to pursue a detailed examination of trumpet-making techniques if the information gained will be only of academic interest. It is the aim of
this book to describe as accurately and completely as possible how trumpets were
made in the city of Nuremberg during their classic period—what tools were needed,
what materials were used and where they came from, and how this raw stuff was
transformed into highly efficient and decorative musical instruments. But also, and
of equal importance, it is intended by inference to describe how they should be
made today, with the intention of achieving a better musical result.

The technique of *making* an early trumpet correctly is no more inaccessible to us
than the technique of *playing* it correctly. There is no magic; there are no lost arts.
There is nothing which cannot be relearned in the same manner as it was learned
in the past. Like the musician, the maker, too, must make himself at home in his
predecessor's workshop and be conversant with the tools, techniques, and materials he finds there. It is as difficult for a metalworker, brought up with modern in-
dustrially produced materials and relatively sophisticated tools, to set himself back
two centuries as it is for the player nurtured on modern mouthpieces and valves to
do the same. Nevertheless, the premise upon which this book is based is simply that
there is but one way to do the job—the original way.

Sources of Information

Nuremberg has been chosen as the focus of this study for several reasons. Primarily, the sheer number and variety of surviving instruments from the city's workshops provide ample material for examination and analysis. Also, documentation of
the industry is more complete than in other, less productive centres. Nevertheless,
because of its huge output and well-established production methods, it is likely that
the construction techniques of Nuremberg instruments provided models for other
smaller centres to emulate. While there are abundant regional variations in decoration and style, metalworking technique appears more uniform. Thus, conclusions
drawn concerning production of Nuremberg trumpets may be equally applicable to
instruments of other centres.

The trumpet-makers also produced other instruments including trombones,
horns, and a variety of special orders and presentation pieces. Although this book
concentrates almost exclusively on trumpets, it can be assumed that other instruments would have been built with essentially similar techniques.

Because metal is malleable and ductile it lends itself more readily to mechanical
processing techniques than, for example, wood or other organic materials. And
when machine mass production is fully established, memory of the old hand techniques becomes at least partially lost. This was the case when industrial methods

began to be applied at the close of the eighteenth century. In the manufacture of brass instruments hand-work of one sort or another continued even in factories where mechanical techniques were widespread. For example, although bells might have been finish-formed by spinning or hydraulic pressure in the factory, they were still cut out, seamed, and rough shaped by hand. Nevertheless, mass-production techniques which relied upon machines made many of the finer and more labour-intensive jobs obsolete and greatly modified the remaining hand techniques. So, while the original techniques are by no means lost, they are obscured under layers of later adaptation.

There are three possible avenues of research when reconstructing the techniques used to make an artefact: examination of the work of living craftsmen, contemporary literary sources, and tool marks and other evidence on extant examples. This is approximately an ascending order of reliability. These three are are discussed in the following sections.

Living Tradition

The work of living craftsmen is traditionally an excellent guide to early techniques provided that a reliable lineage of production can be clearly established. In the case of brass instruments this is not possible; mechanical techniques have been applied universally for well over two centuries. The hand techniques may, therefore, have become considerably modified or lost altogether. The work of repairers and restorers is of particular interest to this study because they are obliged to recreate where possible the finished appearance and performance of the original. However, it is misleading to place too much reliance on living technique as even the most basic hand-tool work, when applied to specific artefacts, can become modified or misapplied over the course of time. Two typical cases illustrate this point: it has been reported that bells of instruments were traditionally thinned down with a scraper (see Chapter 6, under 'The Bell') although this is actually the application of a modern repairer's technique; and lathe spinning for shaping bells and bell garlands has been advocated by modern makers although there is no evidence that the smiths of Nuremberg found it possible, or were even permitted by their internal guild rules to do so.

Literary Sources

Literary sources specific to trumpet-making in Nuremberg are scarce. The craftsmen themselves were generally illiterate, the sum of their book learning being the facility to figure costs and, if high enough in the hierarchy, to make the accounts balance and answer correspondence. They had neither the education nor the time to describe the intricacies of their craft, and were in all probability quite secretive. The chief description of their craft was written by a third party with little understanding of the processes and no necessity to elaborate on them. At first glance the section on the *Trompetenmacher* in Christoph Weigel's *Abbildung der gemein nützlichen Hauptstände*, published in Regensburg in 1698, seems most helpful, but his description of how the work is done may be translated as follows:

The trumpet-maker has first to cut silver and brass, as well as copper, sheets appropriately, and has to join and solder them with utmost neatness and beat them on the anvil and stake. When working with silver, one has to use good [*probe*] silver which is melted and poured into a mould and subsequently beaten to a thin sheet with the hammer and, when it is worked—as mentioned before for brass and copper—is annealed to a white colour. Then the ornaments are soldered on and it is gilded most beautifully.[2] (pp. 233–4.)

There is nothing in this statement which cannot be derived from a cursory examination of an instrument and a bit of common sense, but a deeper explanation is not the point of Weigel's book. It serves its chief purpose as an article of propaganda—it is a very early example of a chamber of commerce brochure and as mere advertising it is less misleading than most. For the student of trumpet-making technique it is not useful. The illustration which accompanies the text (see Fig. 30) is often reproduced in modern studies, but its several shortcomings have not been discussed in any detail.[3] It was clearly not drawn from life, but is rather a reconstruction of an impression (which is of course quite adequate to its task).

The *Encyclopédie* of Diderot and d'Alembert contains a section on brass instrument-making and, although published in Paris from 1751 onwards, there are striking similarities between the tools illustrated and those shown by Weigel (see Fig. 31). This should not be surprising considering the universality of tools and the fundamental nature of most techniques. Unfortunately, the illustration deals primarily with the making of horns. Incidentally, the lowly status of the trumpet-maker is made plain by his inclusion in the section on the *Chaudronnier*—the maker of cauldrons.

A further useful source of information on the trumpet-maker's tools are the two illustrations published in Augsburg in 1740 by Martin Engelbrecht (see Figs. 32 and 33). They show the *Trompeten, Posaunen und Waldhornmacher* and the *Trompe-*

---

[2] *Es muß aber der Trompeten-Macher zu seiner Arbeit | so wohl die Silberne als aus Messing und Kupffer gemachte Bleche | erstlich zu recht schneiden | auf das netteste zu sammen fügen | mit guter Vor-sich tigkeit löthen | richten | und auf dem Ambos und Becher-Eisen heraus schlagen. Zu der silbernen Arbeit muß man gutes Prob-Silber schmelzen | so dann in einen hiezu dienlichen Einguß | ausgiessen | mit dem Hammer zu einem dinnen Blech schlagen | und wan es auf oberzehlte Art | wie wir gleich zuvor von dem Messing und Kupffer gesagt | gearbeitet worden | wieder weiß gesotten | die Zieraten aufgelöthet | und auf das schönste verguldet werden.*

[3] Wörthmüller ('Trompeten- und Posaunenmacher', 378–9) discusses the tools in some detail and his inventory, although not that of a metalworker, is largely complete.

tenmacherin and, although slightly bizarre in appearance, they both contain a wealth of information on the tools and other apparatus, while also showing equipment that neither Diderot nor Weigel includes. All the above illustrations are examined in detail in Chapter 5, under 'The Workshop'.

Another potential source of information is the *Handwerksordnung der Trompeten-macher* which are preserved in the City Archives of Nuremberg. The documents lay down the trumpet-maker's rules and regulations and occasionally throw up asides on technique or quality control. Wörthmüller has provided an extremely useful synopsis of this material ('Die Nürnberger Trompeten- und Posaunenmacher', 281–92).

In spite of the paucity of specific information on tools and techniques, the trumpet should not be seen in isolation from other artefacts produced in similar workshops at the same time. The makers of brass musical-instruments shared tools, techniques, and suppliers with many other metalworking crafts and trades in Nuremberg, so it should not be surprising to find similarities in stock materials, forming and joining techniques, and decorative details. For this reason, other sources on general metalworking techniques may also be consulted. For example, the *Ständebuch* of Jost Amman and Hans Sachs (1568) contains many illustrations of tools and techniques which the trumpet-makers shared. The poetry is execrable.

Tool Marks

Tool marks on the surface of instruments, and metallographic analysis where feasible, provide the most reliable evidence for reconstruction of techniques. If interpreted correctly the evidence is irrefutable. The study of tool marks on trumpets is assisted by two very useful circumstances: firstly, the techniques varied hardly at all over the entire Nuremberg brass-instrument period and, secondly, crude finishing during the decline of the craft left copious tool marks. Nevertheless, interpretation of the surface appearance of an instrument must take into account three possible mechanisms whereby original features may be altered or obliterated.

1. During manufacture: when a forming technique requires two or more processes the second process may obliterate traces of the first, the third the second, and so on. For a fairly obvious example, the primary hammer marks made in forming the bell will almost certainly be obscured by the secondary burnishing treatment.

2. In normal use: abrasive polishing employed when the instrument was in use will have removed evidence of manufacturing technique. Engraved and embossed details on some instruments are noticeably softened by repeated polishing; tool marks will often have disappeared as well. Similarly, wear due to handling is often seen, particularly on the cross stays of trombone slides.

3. During repair and restoration: while still in use or (unfortunately) while in the care of collectors or museums, many characteristic features can be altered or obliterated. Common restoration techniques like dent removal and polishing invariably obliterate evidence. Certain recent restorations of trumpets in museum collections have resulted in objects of dazzling beauty—obtained, paradoxically, at the cost of historical value.

Even though correct and systematic reconstruction of early trumpets must take living tradition, literary sources, and tool marks into account, there is still a corner reserved for intuition. Perhaps the guiding principle should be that the scholarly pursuits must act as moderators to the craftsmanly instincts. We should not forget that, when all else fails, the hands do have the innate sense to inform the brain.

2

The Instrument and its History

A sovereign may have ever so good an orchestra, venery, royal stables, and other
such ministrations, [but] if he does not retain at least one choir of trumpeters
and kettledrummers, there is, in my opinion, something lacking in the perfection of his household.

Johann Ernst Altenberg

The Nuremberg Trumpet

Before examining the development and progress of the metal industry in Nuremberg it would be advisable first to describe the typical musical instrument which the
trumpet-makers produced in huge quantities for nearly four hundred years. The
classic trumpet is one of the simplest and most uncomplicated instruments in European music. It consists solely of a length of tubing (usually brass) which is folded
upon itself once, runs parallel for three-quarters of its length, and then flares outwards into a bell for the remainder. The tubing is about 10 or 12 mm. in diameter
and about 2 m. long. As a general rule, the bell expands to ten times the diameter
of the tubing. It is a natural instrument, having no slides, no tone holes, and no
valves or keys. It requires no tuning or voicing during manufacture, apart from
minor adjustments to its length. It is capable of sounding only the notes of the natural harmonic series, except under special circumstances.

Pitch

Two of the four extant sixteenth-century Nuremberg trumpets are reported to be
in very high pitches compared with those of the following century, although this
alone does not indicate a general trend. There are far too few instruments in existence to draw any conclusion from that source. However, Cesare Bendinelli, who
wrote *Tutta l'arte della Trombetta* around 1614, probably played on the 1585
Schnitzer trumpet now in the Accademia Filarmonica in Verona. In his manuscript
he writes for an instrument in C, but this particular instrument is short enough to
stand in F. Its pitch has been specified as E at A=445Hz (*Die Trompete*, 10). At the

beginning of the seventeenth century a pitch of D is specified by Michael Praetorius, the German author of *Syntagma Musicum* of 1619. The adoption, in that century, of at least two separate pitch standards—*Cammerton* for instrumental work and *Chorton*, the old German organ pitch—makes the picture confusing, especially as *Cammerton* itself was adjusted in the early eighteenth century to bring it a full tone above *Chorton* (Baines, *Brass Instruments*, 124–9).[1] The range of eighteenth-century instruments extends in both directions to include trumpets in *Cammerton* B flat at the lower end, and E flat, E, and even F at the upper end. Measuring the pitch of ancient instruments fails to clarify the issue completely as the makers often finished their instruments sharp, and crooks and tuning bits were supplied for making adjustments. Few original examples of early crooks and bits survive. Instruments were also cut down during their working life to raise their pitch and occasionally lengthened to lower it.[2] Also, many of the instruments now in museums may be individual examples of ones made in batches for military or court use and it is apparent that, provided there was consistency *within the set*, the actual pitch may not have been critical. The cavalry generally appear to have preferred a higher pitch, possibly because this made the standard single-wound trumpet a little less ungainly; they were certainly very eager to adopt the double-wound form when it became generally available in the late eighteenth century. All of this results in a diversity of measured lengths and actual pitches of extant instruments and it is occasionally not possible to ascribe an accurate original pitch to a given instrument with any certainty. Johann Ernst Altenburg sums it up in *Versuch* of 1795 when he says 'trumpets made by different makers rarely sound perfectly in tune together, although other causes are responsible for this' (p. 9).[3]

Layout

The parts of the trumpet have been named in various ways over the years, and there is as yet no standard terminology in general use. The terms used in this book follow approximately the nomenclature used by James Talbot in the seventeenth cen-

---

[1] Baines (*Brass Instruments*) takes the explanation of trumpet pitches about as far as it needs to go here, given the evidence of existing instruments. He provides an excellent chart of the tube lengths and possible pitches of some sixty instruments. The chart indicates groupings of instruments around high and low *Cammerton* D, and a further group, probably military, around E flat. There are, however, many anomalous instruments even in his comparatively small sample group.

[2] For example, an instrument by Geyer of Vienna, now in the Carl Claudius' Samling in Copenhagen (F 88), has been cut down from a longer instrument. Described as 'lovely' in an exhibition catalogue of 1980, it is in fact a sadly truncated affair and quite likely acoustically unsound as the ratio of parallel tubing to flare has been altered. An extremely long instrument by Friedrich Ehe, now in the Germanisches Nationalmuseum in Nuremberg (MIR 108), is an ungainly and rather crudely extended instrument of originally much higher pitch.

[3] All quotations from Altenburg throughout this book are taken from E. H. Tarr's translation.

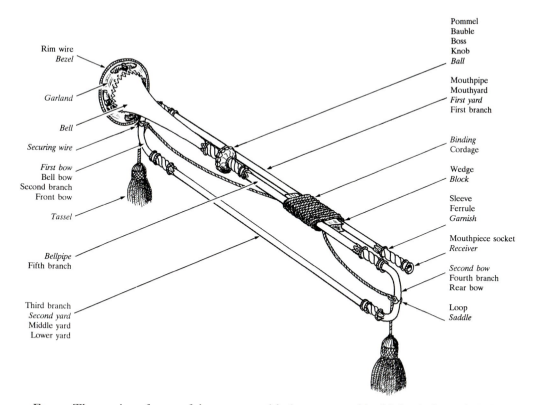

Rim wire
Bezel

Garland

Bell

Securing wire

First bow
Bell bow
Second branch
Front bow

Tassel

Bellpipe
Fifth branch

Third branch
Second yard
Middle yard
Lower yard

Pommel
Bauble
Boss
Knob
Ball

Mouthpipe
Mouthyard
First yard
First branch

Binding
Cordage

Wedge
Block

Sleeve
Ferrule
Garnish

Mouthpiece socket
Receiver

Second bow
Fourth branch
Rear bow

Loop
Saddle

FIG. 1. The naming of parts of the trumpet with the terms used in this book shown in italics. The list is by no means complete; this diagram is a plea for the kind of standardized terminology which almost all other instruments possess

tury with the substitution of bell for 'pavillion', the more descriptive ball for 'boss', and several other more modern terms. Fig. 1 shows the wide variety of ways of naming trumpet parts, with the the terms used in this book shown in italics.

In layout the trumpet consists of the first yard, also called leadpipe, mouthpipe, or mouthpiece yard, which is joined to a U-shaped bow causing the next yard, the middle or second yard, to double back. Another bow doubles back again, joining the second yard to the bellpipe and bell. Expansion begins with the bellpipe and continues through the bell. The bellpipe has a conical cross-section, while the expansion flares outwards in the bell. Although separately designated, the bellpipe and bell are generally made from one continuous piece. (Occasional exceptions are encountered.) All other components are detachable by means of tapered joints. This is the explanation for the trumpets 'all broke to pieces' in English sources. These joints were so often soldered up later in the life of German instruments that it was believed until quite recently that the idea of dismountable components was uniquely English. The joints between components are strengthened with garnishes, or ferrules, which double the thickness of the metal in those areas more prone to damage while also offering sites for decoration and embellishment.

A ball, or boss, usually detachable, is located where the bellpipe blends into the bell. The ball is hollow and is soldered on to a short piece of tubing—a sleeve—which is in turn a snug friction fit over the bell/bellpipe at the correct place. Occasionally two short pieces of tubing are used instead of one continuous piece. The mouthpipe and bellpipe are bound together with fabric tape and cords wrapped around a wooden spacer block which provides a hand hold mid-way between the mouthpiece and the ball. The first yard usually lies to the right of the bell from the player's perspective and the first bow (front bow) is almost always held loosely to the bell by a wire passed through a hole punched in the bellrim and twisted around the saddle on the inner curve of the bow. The strengthening garland around the thin outer edge of the bell carries engraved motifs, and occasionally cast or embossed decorations, and may include such information as the maker's name, his mark, the city where the instrument was made, and the date. The end of the mouthpipe is tapered internally to receive the shank of the mouthpiece, which is almost always a separate item. Excluding the mouthpiece, the standard trumpet is assembled from fourteen separate components: one bell/bellpipe, two yards, two bows, two saddles, five garnishes, one bell garland, and one ball.

Such is the trumpet in the form which arose in the late Renaissance and which persisted well into the nineteenth century. The instrument has such a fundamental simplicity that it is easy to see why, until the advent of keys in the late eighteenth century and valves at the beginning of the next, little variation upon its basic layout was made.[4] Perhaps the achievement of what amounted to perfection in form and function at a comparatively early date instilled in the makers a collective conservatism which was hard to upset when the full impact of the Industrial Revolution began to be felt on the musical-instrument industry.

---

[4] There exist a few anomalous instruments such as the two double-wound trumpets by Ehe in Leipzig and certain coiled instruments which are usually regarded as trumpets. Other variations include the box trumpets by Buchschwinder (one in the Germanisches Nationalmuseum and the other in the Staatliches Institut für Musikforschung in Berlin) where the entire length of tubing is enclosed in a brass cannister. These variations are all of minor importance, by far the vast majority of extant trumpets being in the characteristic once-looped form.

The Brass Industry in Nuremberg

Early History

The supply of raw materials at competitive prices is the key to any successful and enduring industry. The rapid development of Nuremberg brass instrument production between the sixteenth and eighteenth centuries is a symptom of a greater prosperity throughout the metal industry. The industry was catalysed by an increased flow of raw materials, particularly copper, which came about as a result of a change in the pattern of trade at the close of the Middle Ages. Hitherto, international trade in copper had been monopolized by the merchants of the Hanseatic League, a maritime amalgamation of some eighty or more cities along the coasts of Germany and the Low Countries, and north east to the Baltic and Scandinavia. The chief source of copper was the Swedish mines at Falun which had been in existence since at least the twelfth century. The mines in central Europe, away from the north-oriented trade routes, were developed by emigrant Saxon miners from the thirteenth century onwards, but could not achieve international prominence while the towns of the Hanse monopolized the north.

Calamine, the chief ore of zinc used in the production of brass, came principally from Stolberg and Altenberg in the Meuse region of what is now the border of eastern Belgium with Germany. Because of the large bulk of calamine required in the brass-making process it made economic sense to ship refined copper, produced by smelters close to the source, to the region of the calamine deposits. Thus brass-making during the hegemony of the Hanseatic League tended to be concentrated in the north. Aachen, Dinant, and Liège were among the cities of the region which produced brassware in copious quantities. The town of Dinant was particularly well sited and was noted above the others for the production of brass artefacts of all kinds.[5]

The mercantile monopoly of the Hanseatic League began to weaken in the fifteenth century due to internal dissent. The aggressive protectionism of League members resulted in such friction that trading partners were set against each other.

---

[5] There has even been the suggestion (Downey, 26) that the folded form of the trumpet may have been developed by the brass instrument makers of the north, perhaps in Burgundy or France, in the 14th cent. The oft-quoted contention that trumpet-makers 'invented' the technique of bending tubes, whether in Nuremberg or somewhere in the north, seems to have acquired the status of fact. However, no metalworker with a historical bent would accept such a statement at face value. Evidence for the existence of antique instruments with bent tubing, as opposed to castings, is scant. However, Smithers says: 'there is no doubt that the Romans were capable of bending metal tubes' (*Baroque Trumpet*, 335), which suggests that trumpets of the twice-folded, or once-looped, variety may have an unbroken lineage from Classical times.

Lithuania and Poland, which lay upon the ancient and prosperous trade route through Novgorod to the Near East, broke away from the League at the end of the fourteenth century, and only a few years later the Scandinavian countries were in open conflict with the German states. During Burgundian expansion Dinant was sacked in 1466 by Phillippe III. It never recovered its former position as an industrial centre, although brass work on a minor scale continued, and is a tradition of the region to this day.

Meanwhile, the overland trade routes for copper between central European mines and the port of Antwerp came to be regarded by entrepreneurs as economically feasible and worth developing. Nuremberg lay conveniently on such an inland route and had for centuries been the commercial and cultural centre of the southern German region. The city, straddling the River Pegnitz in the heartland of Franconia, had achieved imperial status in the thirteenth century. It received its charter in 1219 and the first town council sat in session in 1256. Although the Holy Roman Empire never had a fixed seat, the city was the favoured *Standquartier* of all German kings and emperors for five hundred years. It was a centre of learning and of the arts, and a manufactory of an enormous variety of the accoutrements of nobility, war, science, and navigation. Nuremberg boasted painters like Michael Wohlgemuth (his illustration of Nuremberg appears in Fig. 2) and his pupil, the incomparable Albrecht Dürer, sculptors of the calibre of Veit Stoss who worked in wood, Adam Kraft the stonemason, and Peter Vischer the brass founder. The gamut of craftsmen in metal, glass, ceramics, wood, and textiles is illustrated in the 1568 *Ständebuch* of Jost Amman and Hans Sachs, the cobbler-poet. Nuremberg's art and artists became renowned throughout Europe. The philosophical disciplines were represented by the humanist Willibald Pirkheimer and Philipp Melanchton, who founded the Gymnasium in 1526, the year after the adoption by the city of the tenets of the Reformation. The astronomer Regiomontanus was resident in Nuremberg, and so was Martin Behaim, the designer of the first terrestrial globe.

The city's further rise to an international prominence in metalworking could not have occurred had there not already been a thriving industry from earlier times. Indeed, the *Beckenschläger*, or basin beaters, of Nuremberg are first mentioned in the town records of 1373 (Haedeke, 76) and guilds for a wide variety of crafts existed long before the demise of the Hanseatic League. A metal industry of some kind had very probably existed in Nuremberg since antique times. The demand for raw materials, particularly metals, once catered for by aggressive and cost effective marketing, stimulated the further growth of already productive industries.

The Fugger family of Augsberg, a dynasty of merchants, bankers, and financiers, were largely responsible for the new central European axis of trade in copper, and Nuremberg very quickly became the centre of their operations, (Ball, 106–10). An office was established in the city by the Fuggers in 1486. The metal came from

Fig. 2. The city of Nuremberg from the south-east in 1493, from Michael Wohlgemut's woodcut in *Liber Cronicarum* of Hartmann Schedel. (As the illustration crosses the centre fold of the book, it has been retouched in this copy to enhance its appearance)

mines in the Tyrol, and from Neusohl in Slovakia (now Banská Bystrica) over which Jakob Fugger had acquired a controlling interest in 1495. An idea of Fugger's worth can be gained by his ability to lend Charles V the wherewithal to purchase the crown of Holy Roman Emperor. A merchant who could command such wealth was a power indeed; Albrecht Dürer's portrait captures the essence of the man.[6] Further to the Fugger interests in copper, an agreement between Nuremberg and Mansfeld was signed in 1502 assuring an outlet for and stimulus to the copper producers of the Harz Mountains. This also ensured a continuing supply of copper after Anton Fugger, son of Jakob, relinquished his hold on the market in 1547. Nuremberg was also supplied with copper from mines in the Erzgebirge.

The increase in trade and the development of more efficient means of transportation made it no longer necessary to situate the brass works near the source of the ores. Calamine could be shipped to Nuremberg from the Meuse Valley by river barges, or road where necessary. The Pegnitz was never navigable, although it was

---

[6] This portrait is in the possession of the Bayerische Staatsgemäldesammlungen in Munich and was, until recently, on display in the Alte Pinakothek.

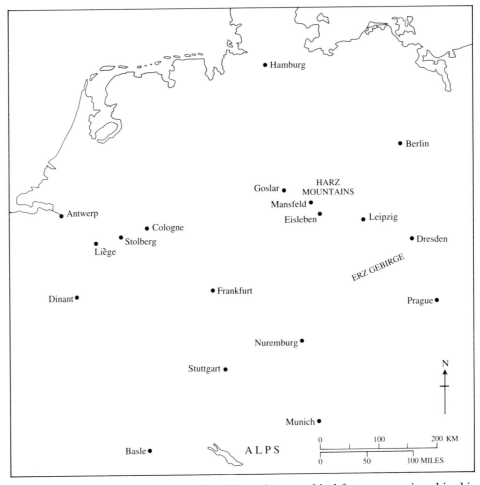

FIG. 3. Map of Central Europe showing cities and geographical features mentioned in this book

used from early times for powering machinery. The name of the village of Hammer, a few kilometres upriver, recalls the use of water-powered machinery; the remains of a flume can still be seen. It became possible for industrial centres like Nuremberg to establish their own plants for producing the alloy and also for hammering it into slabs, sheets, and bars suitable for the local craftsmen. The mining, smelting, and refining of copper and silver, and the production of sheet metal for the musical-instrument industry, are discussed in Chapter 3.

Perhaps of equal importance to the developing industry was the flow of knowledge and expertise which the increased trade in metals and other commodities across the Alps brought with it. Routes between Venice and Trieste in the south, and the northern ports of Antwerp and Amsterdam, passed through Nuremberg. By the close of the fifteenth century materials and expertise, artistic ideas and published works, flowed into the city to be consumed and transformed by an industry which was establishing extensive markets for its products throughout Europe. The manufacture of scientific, mathematical, and musical instruments in brass achieved particular prominence.

The Makers and their Instruments

It is known that trumpets were being made in Nuremberg in the late fifteenth century; the town records of Frankfurt-on-Main, for example, report the purchase of instruments in 1490 or 1491 (Baines, *Brass Instruments*, 104). These were arguably not the products of a fledgling industry and it is likely that, to be exporting instruments some distance to the north, the industry was already well known and firmly established. Initally, the trumpet-makers did not have an independent guild of their own, but were enrolled in the Guild of the Coppersmiths (Wörthmüller, 'Trompeten- und Posaunenmacher', 212).[7] Despite the name, this was a wide-ranging discipline and the embrace of the trumpet-makers, and the privileges that membership bestowed, is indication of their small numbers and low production, rather than lowly status. It was in the early sixteenth century that the trumpet-makers split from the Coppersmiths and inaugurated their own guild of specialists. Trumpet-making was a family affair; in the entire span of the Nuremberg brass instrument industry there are only about twenty-five names and the great families number only eight or nine. Two families stand out for their longevity, the quality of their work, and the number of instruments they produced. The Ehe family were brass-instrument-makers from shortly after 1600 until almost the end of the eighteenth century, and the Haas spanned four generations in the seventeenth and eighteenthth centuries. Between them they account for a huge proportion of the instruments now extant.

The Sixteenth Century

The earliest Nuremberg brass instrument family known by name are the trumpet and trombone-makers, the Neuschels. Hans and his brother Leinhard were working at the end of the fifteenth century and it is likely that their father, Hans the

---

[7] Wörthmüller's two works on the history of the brass instrument industry in Nuremberg are invaluable and so far unsurpassed.

Elder, was also a trumpet-maker. Hans won the praises of the Emperor Maximillian I and personally presented a silver trombone to Pope Leo X. The young Hans' son, Georg, carried on the family business, producing a variety of wind instruments in wood as well as metal. He was the last of the Neuschel line and died in 1557 (Wörthmüller, 'Die Nürnberger Trompeten- und Posaunenmacher', 212). No trumpets of the Neuschel family have survived.

The second famous sixteenth-century family were the Schnitzers. The patriarch, Albrecht, came from Augsburg at the close of the fifteenth century. His sons, Erasmus and Hans the Elder, both of whom died in 1566, became trumpet-makers of some reputation. A trombone by Erasmus dated 1551, now in the Germanisches Nationalmuseum (MI–170), is the earliest known Nuremberg brass instrument, although the actual parts which date from that time are few (Fischer, *HBSJ* 73). Sigmund and Hans the Younger, the other sons of Albrecht, were noteworthy musicians, as were the sons of Hans the Elder, Veit and Hans. Another branch of the family produced Anton Schnitzer, a wealthy burger who was nominated to the town council in 1596. There were apparently two sons, Anton the Younger and Jobst, and the family tradition ended with Anton's son Eberhard in the seventeenth century (Wörthmüller, 'Die Nürnberger Trompeten- und Posaunenmacher', 212–13).

STYLISTIC FEATURES

There are only four extant Nuremberg trumpets from the sixteenth century and all carry the name of Anton Schnitzer, although it is unclear which are by the father and which the son. These include the famous serpentine instrument made for Cesare Bendinelli, now in the Accademia Filarmonica in Verona, another serpentine instrument in the possession of the Gesellschaft der Musikfreunde in Vienna (Fig. 4), an instrument of silver in the usual single-looped form, in the Kunsthistorisches Museum in Vienna (Fig. 5) and one in brass in the Musée Instrumental of the Paris Conservatory. All these surviving instruments are highly decorated and beautifully finished, and were very obviously special commissions. They doubtless give a biased view of the typical instrument of the period. There is always the suspicion that function can give way to form; that the decorative aspect might be considered more important than mere utility. The use of silver is a case in point—its value and decorative quality far outweigh its usefulness as a material for making good musical instruments. The Paris instrument, made of brass and in the 'standard' form, is the most typical of the period.

We cannot know if the Schnitzer and their contemporaries also produced the more utilitarian military-style instruments, but it is possible. The elaborate commissions, often in precious metals, are more likely to survive as treasured items than

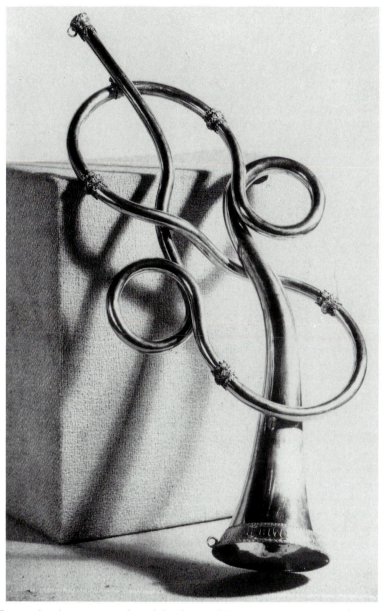

FIG. 4. Serpentine instrument of 1598 by Anton Schnitzer. Even though two of the four surviving 16th-cent. instruments are of this shape, contemporary illustrations indicate that this bizarre form was actually quite rare. This shape is often described as 'pretzel', even in the literature. Pretzels are, of course, shaped nothing like this. The term 'serpentine' indicates a fluidity of shape without evoking a particular geometrical form. (Gesellschaft der Musikfreunde, Vienna, No. 181)

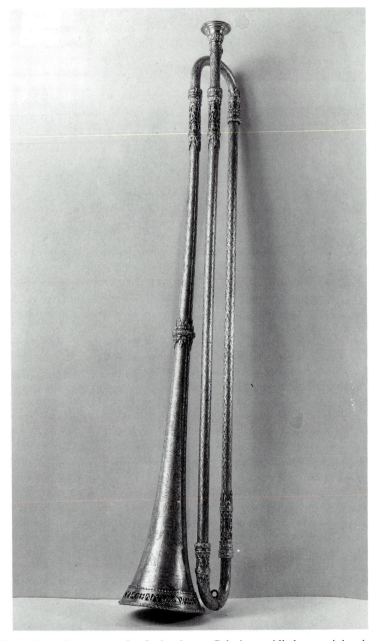

FIG. 5. Single looped trumpet of 1581 by Anton Schnitzer. All the surviving instruments of the 16th-cent. are as beautifully finished and decorated as this one, and undoubtedly masterworks made for special occasions. (Kunsthistorisches Museum, Vienna, Sammlung alter Musikinstrumente, No. 248)

the plain brass instruments which, once out of fashion and beyond economical repair, still had a certain scrap value. Cheaper, unadorned instruments for town bands or military use must have been offered for sale by some, perhaps now unknown, makers, but a representative example has simply failed to survive. Though it is pointless to speculate at this early stage in the instrument's history, one does wonder if apprentices and journeymen in the workshops produced the utilitarian work and even formed and rough finished parts for the masters' commissions.[8] It is not until a century or more later that one can clearly identify two distinct qualities of instruments by the Nuremberg makers, but the practice may have had long antecedents. Alternatively, the trumpet-makers of these two early families may have had the luxury to pursue only valuable and reputable commissions, like the renowned artists of other disciplines. If this is the case, the roots of their craft must lie very deep in history, because such a reputation does not come easily.

The decorative features of the three surviving elaborate instruments may not be typical, but the general dimensions and manner of construction of the one single-looped brass example in Paris probably are. It is interesting to note that from the earliest existing Nuremberg instrument to the last examples of the nineteenth century, the general features of construction, and the techniques employed, vary hardly at all. The sixteenth-century trumpet featured the distinctive long-short-long-short-long arrangement of garnishes which never varied,[9] the bows already had a 'standard' curvature bringing the yards approximately 8 cm. between centres, and even the bell seam with its characteristic square tabs was still made the same way three centuries later. The bell of the sixteenth-century instrument is its chief distinguishing feature; it has a comparatively shallow flare[10] which tends to give stability and good intonation to the lower harmonics and produces a rich and luxurious sound. There is a small 'ball' approximately halfway along the bell (between bell and bellpipe) but it has yet to develop into the substantial feature of later trumpets. Neither of the surviving single-looped instruments has a spacer block or cord ties between the bellpipe and first yard. In fact, the beautiful punched and engraved designs on the tubes of the 1581 instrument would be covered in part if bindings had existed. Contemporary illustrations of trumpet players often show both tubes

---

[8] There are practical reasons why this might be so. 'The Workspace and Working Conditions' in Chapter 5 discuss the daily operations of the workshop and its rather unpleasant environment.

[9] The Schnitzer trumpet in Paris has suffered a rearrangement of its garnishes—it now has two short ones on the front bow.

[10] The term 'funnel shaped' seems to have become the normal description for the bells of early trumpets and trombones. This is curious because a funnel is normally entirely cylindrical, unless one is referring to a device for directing fluids into narrow-necked containers. However, as Stephen Dedalus is at pains to point out, this is correctly called a tundish. It is by no means shaped like a trumpet bell, being conical in section. The preferred description for the shape of the early trumpet bell ought to be 'shallow flare', 'gradual flare', or something similar.

FIG. 6. Mounted trumpeters gripping their instruments by both yards near the bow. No spacer block is evident. ('Representation of the Procession and Games at the Occasion of the Baptism of the Son of Jean Frederic, Duke of Würtemberg, in Stuttgart, from the 10th to the 17th March, 1616', Matthäus Merian)

being gripped in the hand, and there is no evidence of spacer blocks or other stays, fragile though this arrangement must have been (Fig. 6).

The Seventeenth Century

The zenith of Nuremberg's cultural activity occurred around 1616, at the time when the architect Jakob Wolff had completed work on the Rathaus. But even as the city was celebrating its eminence there was evidence of a coming change in fortunes. The arduous overland trade route which had made the city a centre of commerce came under increasing competition from the newly established sea passages, particularly to the East Indies. The overland trade to the Near East through Italy was gradually lost to Dutch merchant seamen operating from the North Sea ports.

The effect of this gradual attrition was hugely exacerbated by the Thirty Years War, which commenced in earnest in 1618.[11] The deep division of Europe between Lutheranism, Calvinism, and Roman Catholicism was confused by both political and dynastic issues with Germany as its chief battleground. The Habsburg dynasty and the Roman Catholics formed a faction against the German princes and the Bourbons of France. Eventually Spain, the Netherlands, and Scandinavia also became embroiled. Commerce came to a virtual standstill and the market in manufactured commodities dried up for decades. Much of Germany was laid waste and in some cities such court luxuries as stables of musicians and singers became things of the past. Nevertheless, in Nuremberg trumpet workshops continued to produce instruments, as several dated examples in collections attest. There appears to have been no hiatus in production, and perhaps the military demand for instruments accounted for this.

The signing of the Peace of Westphalia in 1648 signalled the beginning of the end of conflict, and in its commercial enterprises Nuremberg was about to embark upon its greatest period. The supply of metals and the market for finished work were still well established and the brass instrument industry showed a large upswing during the last half of the seventeenth century. By virtue of aggressive marketing, cheap raw materials, and, of course, excellent workmanship under rigid quality control, Nuremberg acquired the lion's share of the European market in brass instruments.

STYLISTIC FEATURES

The shallow flared bell and relatively conservative decoration persisted well into the century. It is a mistake to refer to this shape as 'Renaissance' as it persisted in some makers' hands until at least 1650. Of particular interest is a trumpet dated 1632 by Hanns Hainlein, now in the musical-instrument collection of the Stadtmuseum in Munich (Fig. 7). It has very elegant lines and the typical shallow bell flare and wide throat of the brass Schnitzer instrument of thirty-three years earlier. There is very restrained decoration confined to punched designs on the garnishes and simple engraving on the bell garland. The ball is more substantial, but still not as large as it was to become. The rim bezel of this instrument is missing but it doubtless followed Hainlein's pattern, being of semicircular cross-section and having repeating dart designs punched on it.[12] A wooden spacer block with cord binding exists on this instrument, but it is difficult to say when this method of securing first became used; the original and subsequent owners would undoubtedly tie and retie the cords many

---

[11] 'Thirty Years War' is a convenient tag for a conflict which raged long before 1618 and only truly ceased in the 60s of the century.

[12] Wörthmüller and Heyde provide diagrams of the many characteristic punched and engraved patterns used by the Nuremberg masters.

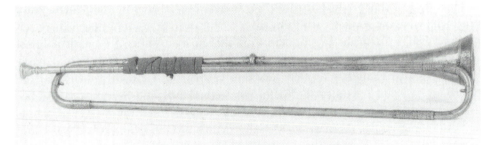

FIG. 7. Trumpet by Hanns Hainlein 1632. This bell has the shallow flare typical of the period and the instrument is generally undecorated. The workmanship is excellent. (Munchener Stadtmuseum—Musikinstrumentenmuseum, No. 67/05)

times. However, from the Michael Nagel trumpet found in the wreck of the Royal Swedish Flagship *Kronan* we know that wood blocks, linen ties, cord bindings, and tassels were in use in 1676, when the ship was lost (Karp, *ICTM* 95–7). All in all, the Hainlein instrument of 1632 is a perhaps more reliable witness to the early seventeenth-century pattern than any decorated one, primarily because it is of brass, is relatively unadorned and is obviously utilitarian.

Around the middle of the seventeenth century a sudden major change in the trumpet occurred. Hitherto, the bell profile had been relatively shallow and the throat fairly wide, but in a short space of time bells with a sharper flare and narrower throat began to appear (Fig. 8). This change coincided with the appearance of more demanding music for the instrument's upper register. Such works as Maurizio Cazzati's compositions for San Petronio in Bologna, Pavel Vejvanovsky's sonatas, and the various trumpet scorings by Jean-Baptiste Lully indicate a new idiomatic treatment of the instrument. Although the trend had been developing since the trumpet corps was first invited to play along with the other musicians in the first decades of the century (e.g. Schütz's 'Danket dem Herren', from the *Psalmen Davids* of 1619, SWV 45) expressive work for the instrument blossomed fully in the 1660s.

The sharper flare of the bell was not brought about by a new technique but was, rather, an adaptation. As noted earlier, the method of seaming the bell remained constant throughout. The increased flare was achieved simply through thinning the metal by more hammering. As a direct result of this thinness the bell garland was required to be wider and also to follow closely the contour of the bell to offer better support. The narrow, conical-section garland was gradually replaced by a wide, flared section probably formed on the same mandrel as the bell itself. This widening led, in turn, to the use of more elaborate decoration. Where previously there was

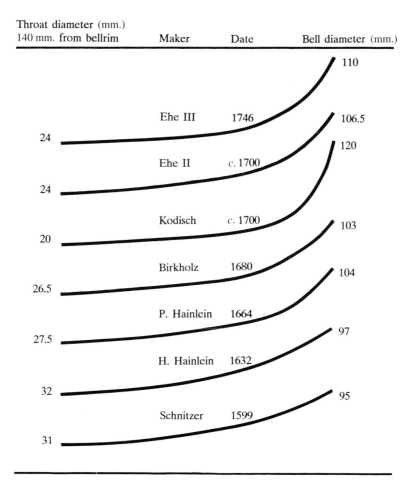

Fig. 8. Comparison of bell profiles from seven Nuremberg instruments. As bell diameter increases, throat diameter generally decreases. The position at which the throat is measured is arbitrary, but remains constant throughout this series. Four distinct classes of profile can be distinguished here: the 'Renaissance' form which was used until the middle of the 17th-cent., the Middle Baroque with slightly increased flare and a narrower throat, a maximum flare with very narrow throat of the Kodisch of around 1700, and the so-called standard form of the Late Baroque. The time periods of all these forms overlap each other, but the Kodisch is somewhat anomalous; a progression from Middle to Late Baroque is clearly evident

space only for the maker's name and his mark (and the town and date, if included) there was now room for more engraving and, in the case of elaborate instruments, embossed scallop-shells and cast angel heads. The decorative elements so characteristic of the classic trumpet arose as a result of a typical Baroque *horror vacui*.

Even though acoustic performance was substantially modified by this reformation, it is apparent that the resonant quality of the metal of the bell itself was not considered a factor. Not only was an extra swathe of metal added to the end in the form of the increased garland, but heavy castings were also added. These are first seen on ceremonial instruments of the 1650s; see, for example the detail of an instrument by Sebastian Hainlein of 1657 in Fig. 54. The increased mass on the end of the bell causes damping to the natural vibrations of the metal, but the comparative acoustic 'deadness' which results was apparently not thought important.

The Eighteenth Century

Other centres had been in production and developed further in this period, notably the workshops in Prague and the Viennese school led by the Leichamschneiders, but most were parochial by comparison. Because of energetic marketing and mass production one finds that Nuremberg-made brass instruments in museums and private collections today outnumber all other contemporary examples by a huge margin. Although owners, players, and connoisseurs of antique instruments might be reluctant to admit that a particular instrument was made by anything less than the personal touch of a master craftsman, it is certain that mass production was in effect. The name engraved around the bell garland only occasionally salutes the craftsman who actually did the work. The name of Johann Wilhelm Haas, for example, was engraved upon all instruments from the family factory long after his death. Smithers observes that: 'It is not impossible to think that, for whatever period of time, one person was assigned to the task of making tubing, another garnishes, etc.' (*Baroque Trumpet*, 337). It is indeed far from impossible; in the sixteenth and seventeenth centuries it is quite likely, and by the eighteenth century it is an absolute certainty that mass production was practised, and was the norm for all but special commissions. The comparatively large number of extant instruments is, of course, a very small fraction of those originally sold. And this large production by a small number of named makers indicates factory-like methods. Although it would be tempting to try to estimate the number of instruments produced by a family workshop in a given time, the figures would have to be based upon the following (perhaps unobtainable) information.

1. Number of employees and breakdown of tasks. How many journeymen would be employed by a specific workshop and were there also employees of lower rank, with no aspiration to rise, whose job it was to produce components? They are not mentioned explicitly in the *Handwerksordnung der Trompetenmacher*, which are the regulations which apply to what might be termed the 'professionals'.

2. Buying in. How many components were bought from stockists and how many were made on site? It is known that castings were produced in large numbers for all craftsmen in specialized foundries; this was also true for stamped rim bezel wire, embossed or rolled garnish decoration, and similar fittings. Engraving was certainly contracted out for the special ceremonial instruments.

3. Type of instrument produced. Did workshops specialize? It is likely that some workshops concentrated on trombones or horns, while others produced a larger proportion of trumpets.

4. Time taken to make an instrument. This is, of course, the most important factor. It depends upon the type of instrument, the quality and the degree and nature of input from all workers involved.

Suffice it to say that from the number and quality of Nuremberg instruments, a persuasive argument can be made for piece-work and production-line assembly. This large turnover of brasses—more so probably than any other musical instrument—is accounted for by the following factors.

1. Unlike wooden wind instruments, metal ones are of fragile construction and are more prone to accidental damage. Damaged parts could be replaced but a crumpled or dented bell (the most commonly observed damage) is usually irreversible.[13]

2. Also, unlike all other musical instruments, brasses have a scrap value once they are beyond economical repair. Recovery of a percentage of purchase price makes recycling attractive.

3. Many trumpets were destined for military use, which is hard on all equipment, especially fairly soft non-ferrous metals.

4. The rapid change of styles in both shape and decoration would soon make court and ceremonial instruments obsolete. Although still of value, they might not be of use.

STYLISTIC FEATURES

The style established in the last decades of the seventeenth century continued well into the following one. On the more elaborate instruments it is not unusual to find garnishes constructed of fluted brass sheet attached to heavy cast end pieces. Engraving covers the garland, and cast angel heads, particularly on the Haas and Kodisch instruments, give an air of Baroque flamboyance.[14] The ball has now

---

[13] One does encounter the occasional bell repair done while in use. For example, one of the pair of instruments by Kodisch in the Germanisches Nationalmuseum has a beautifully fitted crescent-shaped patch in the interior, but the damage was minor and the instrument sufficiently valuable to warrant it.

[14] I am indebted to David Edwards for his suggestion that the angel or cherub heads may in fact be representations of the winged god Aulos. The puffed cheeks on these miniature figures certainly appear to symbolize the wind. They have also been said to represent divine wisdom. They are referred to as angel heads throughout this book.

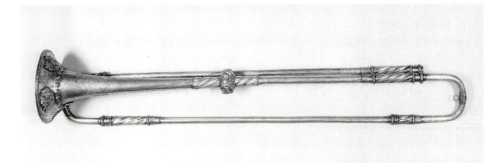

FIG. 9. Silver trumpet by Johann Wilhelm Haas c.1750. A wood block and decorative cordage would have completed the appearance of the instrument. This is the baroque trumpet in its most flamboyant form. Compare the general appearance and workmanship with the illustrations in Figs. 10 and 11 of an instrument from the same workshop. (Metropolitan Museum of Art, New York, No. 54.32.1)

achieved its maximum size. The bellpipe and first yard are bound together with colourful cordage around a wooden spacer block, affording a grip for the right hand. A silver trumpet by Johann Wilhelm Haas, now in the Metropolitan Museum of New York, illustrates the Baroque instrument in its most gorgeous form (Fig. 9). Towards the middle of the century the more sumptuous decoration began to be dropped in favour of a more refined form with cleaner lines. There are two trends at work here: one stylistic and the other economic. The full impact of this change of style is discussed in the next section.

The Decline

The decline of the brass instrument industry in Nuremberg cannot be ascribed to any single factor; it came as a result of a combination of circumstances. The loss of Nuremberg's pre-eminence as a centre of arts and industry, changing musical fashions, and the ever-present guild system, or the mentality underlying it, were the main factors which caused the eventual demise of the industry in the first decades of the nineteenth century.

Nuremberg's cultural zenith had been at the beginning of the seventeenth century but, although the artistic and philosophical soul had left the city by the eighteenth century, its manufacture of commodities continued apace. Contributions to art and learning were slight in comparison. Nuremberg lost its status as a free imperial city in 1806 and came under the sway of Bavaria. By the close of the eighteenth century the industrial fires also began to burn low and the city was only resurrected from mercantile oblivion by the coming of the railways.

By the time of publication in 1795 of the final treatise on the classic trumpet, Altenburg's *Versuch* mentioned earlier, the great days of the natural trumpet were past. The social upheavals of the late eighteenth and early nineteenth centuries led to the dissolution of many small court orchestras and a consequent loss of support for the trumpet specialists they employed. Before the French Revolution and through the Napoleonic years orchestral music underwent its most profound change. It gained mass and volume; it no longer emphasized the idiosyncratic qualities of its individual components, but sought rather to channel and express them in their entirety. The new music demanded participation of the brasses symphonically and their role tended more and more to be relegated to providing a homophonic punctuation. The voice of the trumpet no longer stood out against the orchestra, but underscored it in a purely supporting role. Fluid and intricate works for the trumpet, like the two 'concertos' in two movements by Michael Haydn, are the dying flourishes of the tradition.

The above two factors, the loss of Nuremberg's cultural position and the decline of the trumpet itself, might not alone have spelt the end of the industry—trumpets were still required in the orchestra and the huge social upheavals of the period brought many military orders. Demand was, if anything, increased. But these were trumpets of a different kind. Gone was the flamboyant decoration of the High Baroque, which Altenburg harks back to nostalgically; a trumpet by Haas with cast angel heads on the bell was hopelessly antique by the time his book was published. Gone also was the market for the *kind* of instrument the makers had produced in such quantities and for so long. What was needed was a louder and more robust instrument with a larger bell and thicker metal; a trumpet capable of holding its own in a large orchestra playing to a large audience in a large hall. Why could the brass workers of Nuremberg not respond to these fairly predictable changes in their market?

The final and terminal illness was a stultifying conservatism with which the industry had been imbued by the guild system, and which in the end it was unable to shake off. Henry Crabb Robinson, an English traveller, had this to say of Nuremberg's industry in 1802:

It is the great Toy Shop of almost all Europe And almost exclusively by the Manufactory of Nick-Nacks arose some Centuries since to the rank of one of the first Cities in Europe. It is now a striking picture of fallen & falling Greatness . . . In what respects ingenuity and fineness of Work, the Nurenbergers are still the most dexterous & expert in Europe: Their productions in Brass, their children's toys &c are still unrivalled . . . But as the Nurenbergers are true Goshamites or as the classical phrase here is Abderites—& the great rule of their Conduct is to stand still while the Rest of the World is in progress, their Manufactures re-

main as they were, still of great excellence, but from the change of taste of less demand—
The Birmingham wares are peculiarly injurious to them. (Yapp, 212)

Their dexterity may have been of the finest, but in the application of modern production methods they indeed stood still while the world moved. The chief difference one sees in the Nuremberg instruments of the late eighteenth century and their contemporaries from other centres is that the former are handmade while the latter show the first evidence of machine work.[15] Such mechanical techniques as spinning, drawing, and stamping were being applied to metal manufacture in the first wave of the Industrial Revolution. It was only a matter of time before such techniques were applied to musical instruments. Smoother, straighter tubing could be made with dies and drawplates, bells could be spun in a fraction of the time, and embossed embellishments could be formed in one blow. While there was no longer a demand from the discerning few for handmade instruments, there was a huge market for relatively cheap machine-made ones.

STYLISTIC FEATURES

Hand-made instruments of this period show crudity and haste of construction as if, by sheer numbers, the makers felt able to overcome competition. The instrument shown in Figs. 10 and 11 bears the name of Haas (probably Johann Adam), perhaps the greatest family name of them all, and, although undated, is of late manufacture. On close inspection the workmanship is of a very low standard. The solder seam of the bell is sloppy, the cut-outs between the embossed scallop-shells still bear the marks of the tinsnips, and the burin used to do the engraving has clearly been driven with a hammer instead of guided with the hand. Cast decorations and elaborate garnishes have been dropped in favour of simpler and less labour-intensive construction.

The above impression of craftsmanship in decline is complicated by the fact that two qualities of instrument were always offered. Run-of-the-mill instruments were produced in huge quantities, but the master trumpet-maker still worked on special commissions. It is therefore easy to ascribe journeyman instruments of indifferent workmanship to the period of the decline, especially as so few are dated. Nevertheless, the workmanship seen in Fig. 10 would be unthinkable before the middle of the eighteenth century. By way of contrast, the set of three trumpets of 1746 by Johann Leonhard Ehe III in the Germanisches Nationalmuseum (Fig. 12) show superb workmanship. The clean, uncluttered lines are clearly an expression of a deliberate artistic intent. The decoration of the garnishes is reduced to concentric

---

[15] This somewhat general statement will be enlarged upon later. There is evidence of the use of winch-driven dies for making tubing, and the spinning of bells at the close of the 18th cent. (see Ch. 5, under 'The Workshop').

FIG. 10. Detail of a trumpet from the workshop of Johann Wilhelm Haas, probably late 18th-cent. The hasty construction and crude finishing indicate a journeyman instrument of the late period. (Germanisches Nationalmuseum—Musikinstrumentensammlung, Nuremberg, No. MIR 106)

turnings, the ball is unadorned, and the simple bell garland carries nothing but engraving. In this case the simplification is certainly due to the paring down of Baroque flamboyance in favour of something more austere and neo-classical, but instruments of this quality are rare. The exigencies of mass production play a greater part. The plain, utilitarian lines, visible for example in an early nineteenth century instrument of Christian Wittmann (Fig. 13), have nothing to do with artistic intent; they are quite obviously the result of hasty manufacture.

In the early nineteenth century some time-saving techniques (apart from hasty workmanship) were employed. These can only have been adopted under great economic pressure. For example, the maker's name, I. H. Sterner, on the bell garland of the instrument shown in Fig. 14 has been stamped with letter punches. Also, there is no longer a bezel soldered to the bellrim; the outer edge of the garland has been turned over in the usual way, but a circular wire is trapped inside instead (see

FIG. 11. The solder seam of the Haas trumpet in Fig. 10. If this is the original seam, it is very sloppily done; if it is a later repair, it indicates that the solder joint had failed due to faulty workmanship. (Germanisches Nationalmuseum—Musikinstrumentensammlung, Nuremberg, No. MIR 106)

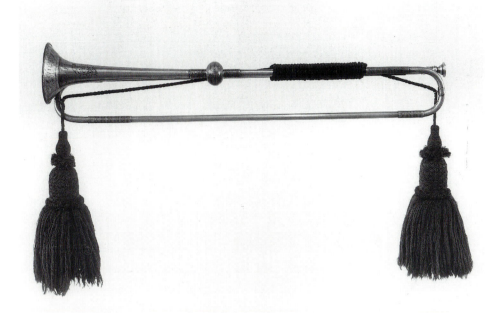

FIG. 12. One of a set of three trumpets by Johann Leonhard Ehe III of 1746. The workmanship on these instruments is superb and obviously that of a master. Decorative details are at a minimum. (Germanisches Nationalmuseum—Musikinstrumentensammlung, Nuremberg, No. MI 217)

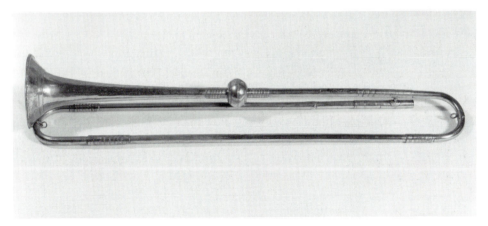

FIG. 13. Early 19th-cent. instrument by Christian Wittmann. The simple lines and lack of decoration are typical. Note the addition of a soldered stay between the first yard and bellpipe, although the bellrim is still held to the front bow by a twisted wire. (Division of Musical History, Smithsonian Institution, Washington, No. 60.1409)

FIG. 14. Detail of the garland of an instrument by Sterner of the early 19th-cent. Letter punches have been used to stamp the name and decorations, and the bellrim is now made by rolling the edge of the garland around a wire. (Author's collection)

Fig. 58). Both these processes are aimed directly at lowering cost of production and they add nothing to the aesthetic effect of the instrument. Wörthmüller says of Sterner's work: 'The simple, almost rationalistic manner of the few decorative details stands in strong contrast to all the instruments of the "older" handcraft' ('Die Instrumente, 470).[16] He mentions another nineteenth-century workshop, that of Johann Christoph Frank, who died in 1818, and his two sons (presumably) Johann Jakob and Johann David.[17] There is a keyed trumpet by Johann Jakob in Leipzig which shows that experimentation did take place, but it is pitifully crude in construction. One wonders whether it was only an experiment or if it really is the sole surviving example of a serious production venture. If the latter, there were better instruments being produced elsewhere. The nineteenth century did not belong to Nuremberg.

[16] *Die einfache, beinache rationalistiche Art des wenigen schmückenden Beiwerks steht im starken Gegensatz zu allen Instrumenten des 'alten' Handwerks.*

[17] There were several other trumpet-makers working in the early 19th cent., including Christian Wittmann, one of whose instruments is illustrated in Fig. 13.

3

The Metal

Since I have no knowledge other than that gained through my own eyes, I tell you as a certainty that just as steel is iron converted by art into almost another kind of metal, so also brass is copper given a yellow colour by art. Surely it was a splendid discovery, for which we must praise the alchemists, although perhaps whoever discovered it was deceived, thinking that he had made gold from copper.

Vannoccio Biringuccio

Brass

Early Terminology

Modern brass is an alloy of copper and zinc in which the proportion of zinc is generally not less than 5 per cent and not greater than 50 per cent. The wide range of alloys falling within these limits are known collectively today as the brasses. They were not always so well defined. It is curious that this material, which was so favoured by musical instrument-makers and other craftsmen, was, from antiquity until well into the the eighteenth century, one of the least understood. The various names under which alloys of copper and zinc have been known show the widespread misunderstanding of its true nature. The Romans referred to all of the copper alloys rather indiscriminately as *aes*, although the term *aurichalcum* was used, for example, by Pliny in his *Natural History* specifically for brass (Book 34.2).[1] The number of brass archaeological artefacts of Roman provenance indicates that it was a fairly popular metal. The twelfth-century monk Theophilus, the first writer to discuss the production of brass in anything like practical detail, uses the same terms *aes* and *aurichalcum* interchangeably.[2]

---

[1] 'Marius copper, also called Cordova copper . . . this kind most readily absorbs *cadmea* and reproduces the excellence of gold-copper in making sesterces and double-as pieces . . .'

[2] In a footnote on p. 143 of Hawthorne and Smith's edition of Theophilus, Smith provides an overview of the often confusing terminology of copper alloys in the Middle Ages.

The word *bræs* occurs in Old English and by the late Middle Ages (to simplify things a good deal) was most often used to denote alloys of copper and tin—which we now know as bronzes. Copper and zinc alloys were generally known as *latten*, a cognate of the French *laiton* and perhaps derived from the Middle High German *latta* meaning a thin plate. (Interestingly, the brass instruments are known today in French as *les cuivres*—the coppers.) It is difficult to generalize on early terminology for brass, as opposed to bronze, because besides the chief metals of these alloys there were often traces of other metals. For example, early specimens of what would have been known as *latten* have been shown to contain considerable amounts of tin and lead. Traces of other metals like iron, nickel and even silver may also exist, due partly to the location of the mines from which the ores came and partly to the widespread propensity for melting scrap into the brass mixture during production.

The root of the German term *Messing* is obscure, but is believed by some to be derived from the Latin *massa*, referring to masses of metal. For the classic period of the Nuremberg trumpet-makers the term *Messing* denotes an alloy of between approximately 10 and 30 per cent zinc in copper. Traces of other elements like iron and lead exist, but not in sufficient quantity to modify this terminology. Lower zinc brasses were also available from the suppliers but do not appear to have been used by the brass-instrument-makers.

To state that brass is an alloy is to apply a modern understanding of it which is quite out of place. Unlike bronze, which was known from prehistory to be an alloy of copper and tin, brass was thought to be copper which had been turned yellow by the influence of an earth, hence the Roman name *aurichalcum* or golden copper. In Classical times this magical earth was called *cadmia*. European names for it are many and varied but in English calamine is by far the most common; in German it is most often known as *Galmei*. The ore is now known by its mineralogical name, smithsonite. The making of brass antedated the alchemy of the Middle Ages, of course, but the ability of calamine to transform red copper into a golden metal accorded well with alchemical philosophy—a metal was heated with an earth causing it to become ennobled, making it more durable and gold-like. (In the same way, iron could be heated with a carbon-bearing earth to ennoble it by making steel.) Calamine is in fact the chief ore of zinc, a metal known but not fully understood until comparatively late in the history of technology.

The absence of zinc, except as a curiosity, from European workshops until the eighteenth century can be blamed primarily upon its volatility. Zinc melts at 419°C and boils at 907°C, but at its smelting temperature (i.e. the temperature at which it is liberated from its oxide) its equilibrium vapour pressure is above that of atmospheric pressure. In other words, at temperatures above about 1,000°C zinc exists as a vapour, making it difficult to detect, let alone smelt and refine. Also, unless a retort is used, in which oxygen is excluded, the zinc vapour will re-oxidize and either condense as zinc oxide on the cooler parts of the furnace, or simply be lost to the atmosphere as smoke.

Paracelsus, writing around the first part of the sixteenth century, is the first writer to refer to zinc by name. He calls it 'A bastard of copper, a peculiar metal, but often adulterated by foreign metals. It is of itself fusible, but does not admit of hammering . . . It does not allow itself to be mixed by art with other metals, but remains by itself'. (Dawkins, 12).[3] The term 'bastard of copper' is not, of course, meant in a derogatory sense; he is simply assigning zinc to the category of half-metals. Bismuth is another such. There were seven true metals known to the alchemists (as there were seven corresponding heavenly bodies)[4] and there was a natural reluctance to turn theory upside-down to include a metal which was thought by most theorists from Classical Greek times onwards to be merely a parody of silver. In *De Re Metallica* of around 1556, Georgius Agricola refers to it as *Conterfei*, a substance of little use which is found as a by-product in lead smelting furnaces. (Agricola, 112). (It is uncertain whether he realized that this was, indeed, zinc.) Elsewhere the term *Conterfeht* is used, the inference being obvious.

In Europe the existence of metallic zinc in any industrial quantity was not known until the beginning of the seventeenth century when ingots were first imported along the silk routes from China. Even then it was not accorded the full status of a true metal. At the beginning of the seventeenth century Löhneiss identified the furnace condensate as a metal, but it was not until 1743 that Marggraf published the method for smelting calamine, the chief ore, to produce zinc (Dawkins, 20). The smelting of zinc ore was first performed on an industrial scale in Europe by William Champion who developed a condensation process around 1738 and patented it in 1740 (Tylecote, *History of Metallurgy*, 132).

The availability of metallic zinc did not immediately displace the calamine process. It was still technically more straightforward to produce brass in the old tried and true fashion, but copper–zinc alloys produced by fusing the two base metals together also became available. Such alloys as pinchbeck (a high zinc brass) and tombac (one with very little zinc) were produced to fulfil certain specific functions; they are hardly met at all in brass musical instruments on the Continent, but in England a red brass was favoured. Copper also began to be used for military instruments in the nineteenth century, although Weigel claims that copper was used by the trumpet-makers of Nuremberg in the late seventeenth century (p. 233).

It would seem reasonable that the existence of zinc, and the ability to alloy it with copper, would lead directly to an understanding of the true nature of brass pro-

---

[3] This passage is taken from Waite's translation. Dawkins provides a very thorough history of the discovery and use of zinc.

[4] The Sun: gold, the Moon: silver, Mercury: mercury, Venus: copper, Mars: iron, Jupiter: tin and Saturn: lead.

duced by the traditional technique. This appears not to be the case. As late as 1760 Johann Georg Friedrich Klein describes the composition of various alloys in his *Beschreibung der Metall-Lothe und Löthungen*. He discusses *Messing* (pp. 68 and 69) 'which is sometimes also called yellow copper'[5] and goes on to say that it 'is made by art, and has as its basis the same copper which through the addition of calamine gives the well-known yellow colour'.[6] Further, he describes mixtures of solders which are made, not from copper and zinc, but from *brass* and zinc. (High zinc brass was made by combining calamine brass with metallic zinc, but this could hardly be the case for small quantities of solder.) The title of Galon's treatise of 1764, *L'Art de convertir le cuivre rouge, ou cuivre en rosette, en laiton ou cuivre jaune*, illustrates the same misunderstanding. It seems clear that Klein and Galon still understand brass to be copper which has been turned yellow, as did the writers of centuries earlier. They therefore make a distinction between brass produced by cementation and the various alloys produced by direct mixing of metals. This shows that, although the craftsmen's intuitive knowledge of the properties and tolerances of their material was of a very high order, their knowledge of exactly what it was they were using was much less well developed.[7]

Manufacture of Brass

The process of making brass in the Renaissance, from the mining of the ores to the finished sheet metal, can be examined in the works of three major authors: the *Pirotechnia* of Vannoccio Birunguccio (1540), *De Re Metallica* and *De Natura Fossilium* of Georgius Agricola (1556 and 1546), and *Beschreibung allefürnemsten mineralischen Ertzt- und Bergwercksarten* of Lazarus Ercker (1580). Although it would be useful to confine the description of the processes closely in both time and place, thus concentrating on Southern Germany between, say, 1600 and 1725, few books of any originality were published on metallurgy in the seventeenth century, reliance being placed on existing and still current editions of the above works. At the close of the seventeenth century a brief description of brass-making appears in Christoph Weigel's *Abbildung der gemein nützlichen Hauptstände* of 1698. In the following century Diderot and d'Alembert's great *Encyclopédie* of *c*.1751 onwards, and Galon's work cited above deal with the subject in great detail.

---

[5] *welcher auch bisweilen gelbes Kupfer genannt wird . . .*

[6] *durch die Kunst gemacht, und ist der Grundtheil desselben Kupfer, welchem durch Zusatz von Galmey die bekannte gelbe Farbe gegeben wird.*

[7] The ignorance of craftsmen of 200 years ago compares very favourably with that of today's instrument makers and players, some of whom have very little idea of what brass actually is. One well-known brass player is quoted in print as saying that 'I have a firm that makes brass for me. They use some substance with trace elements instead of zinc.'

PRODUCTION OF COPPER

The manufacture of brass begins with the mining, smelting, and refining of copper. In *De Re Metallica* Agricola tells us that:

Since Nature usually creates metals in an impure state, mixed with earth, stones and solidified juices, it is necessary to separate most of these impurities from the ores as far as can be, before they are smelted, and therefore I will now describe methods by which the ores are sorted, broken with hammers, burnt, crushed with stamps, ground into powder, sifted, washed, roasted, and calcined (p. 267).

As described in Chapter 2, the copper ore used for Nuremberg brass came from three principal sources: the mines of Slovakia and those in the Harz Mountains and the Erzgebirge. Copper was generally found in various forms of sulphide, including copper glance and copper pyrites. Iron sulphide and other trace metallic sulphides often occurred in the same ore bodies. In prehistoric times copper ore was taken from surface deposits wherever the seams emerged, but within the historical period technical developments made extensive tunnelling possible. The best seams were those that lay on or near a horizontal plane, so that the adit would not slope too steeply. Attack of the seam from the side of a hill was the most convenient approach. In some mines pumps, or at least mechanical bucket lifters, were necessary to keep the workings dry. Removal of ore was done primarily with hammer and chisel, and broken ore was carried to the surface in wheeled tubs. These techniques scarcely changed until the nineteenth century.

Experienced miners, Agricola says, carefully sort the metalliferous rock from the waste during mining. However, it is still necessary to further sort the material above ground for 'to smelt the waste together with an ore involves loss' (p. 268). He suggests too that rock lying close to the ore body also be crushed and examined, especially in areas where the yield is marginal. Occasionally, metals are found in their native state, as sizeable chunks of pure metal. This most commonly occurs with silver in the mines we are concerned with here, but occasionally copper is also found native. These pieces of raw metal were pounded flat with hammers and then cut into pieces in preparation for melting. They would thus bypass the several steps necessary to bring the ore to their purity. For reasons of transportation it made good economic sense to smelt and refine the ore as close to the mines as practicable.

The sorted ore had to be crushed into fairly small pieces before further treatment could take place. Agricola describes several regional (and perhaps mineral) variations on this, from breaking with a hammer while seated at a bench, to smashing with large hammers on the ground. This was followed by sieving and washing. Further on there is a description of iron-shod stampers driven by water power (Fig. 15). These were apparently developed around the beginning of the sixteenth century

FIG. 15. Agricola's illustration of an ore crushing machine which uses iron-shod stampers driven by a water wheel

and, together with improved washing techniques, greatly increased the efficiency of ore extraction.

Both reverberatory and blast-furnaces existed in the sixteenth century for smelting, although Birunguccio is apparently the first to describe the former (p. 281). In a reverberatory furnace air flow for smelting is supplied by natural draught, whereas in the blast-furnace it is supplied by mechanically operated bellows. Birunguccio states that reverberatory furnaces can be preferable as there is less chance of overheating the ore and ruining it (assuming, we suppose, an incompetent operator). A reverberatory furnace, often fired with wood, was generally used for the smelting of softer ores, the blast-furnace being by far the most common for reducing copper ores.

A blast-furnace consists of a vented chamber of fire brick or refractory stone to which is connected an air feed, called a tuyère, from water-powered bellows. At the lowest point of the chamber an outlet leads to a forehearth, a depressed area of the ground lined with clay or fire brick. The outlet, or spigot, to this forehearth is closed with a tile or other refractory substance, which can be removed by means of a long iron hook to allow the furnace to be drained (Fig. 16).

In the first stage of smelting crushed ore was mixed with limestone and charcoal. This was built up in layers within the furnace to a point just below or level with the tuyère. Firing and air blasting commenced until liquid material could be drawn off into the forehearth. The function of this first stage was to smelt out the unwanted fraction of the ore known as gangue, which was mostly silica, and to leave behind concentrated metal sulphides. Where very rich ores were obtained, this first smelting was sometimes unnecessary.

On opening the furnace spigot, the liquid would drain into the forehearth and immediately begin to stratify. The lighter fractions would float to the surface and the heavier materials pool into layers within the depth of the hearth. The slags could often be lifted off the surface as a single, brittle mass. Below this lay matte, a black sulphide containing some iron and as much as 50 per cent copper. As this chilled at the surface it could be lifted off in cakes until, finally, the third layer was reached. This layer (depending upon the nature of the ore) could contain lead, silver and gold. Occasionally, if argentiferous ores were being smelted, and if there was sufficient yield to repay the cost, extra lead was melted into the forehearth before opening the spigot, the better to absorb any silver which the copper might contain. This whole process might be repeated three or four times.

At the completion of the first stage of smelting the contents of the furnace were converted to slags, which were discarded, a large number of cakes of black matte (known in German as *Stein* or *Lech*), and the lower cake of lead and copper with a possible admixture of gold or silver. The latter cake was known as *Werck*, or work lead; the removal of silver from it by liquation and cupellation will be dealt with in a later section.

In the second stage, the matte was crushed and then roasted. Roasting has the function of converting the metallic sulphides to oxides by a simple substitution reaction:

$$Cu_2S + O_2 \text{ (gas)} = 2Cu + SO_2 \text{ (gas)}$$
$$2Cu + O_2 \text{ (gas)} = 2CuO$$

Agricola describes a number of ways of roasting, depending upon location and type of ore. For example, in Eisleben the roasting of copper ore was done by piling the crushed material on to faggots of wood in a conical heap and then firing this from the leeward side, so that it would burn for thirty days or more. In other places a pit was dug and this was filled with alternate layers of ore and wood. In another instance the ore is shown being roasted on perforated iron plates so that the sulphurous and bituminous wastes can be collected underneath in water-filled pots.

FIG. 16. Two blast furnaces illustrated in Agricola's *De Re Metallica*. The forehearths (C) can be seen in front of the furnace aperture. The furnace on the right is in use while the one on the left is shown empty

These waste products, if plentiful enough, were worth collecting for industrial and medicinal uses.

The third stage of smelting required the reduction of the copper oxide to metallic copper. The brittle oxide was broken into pieces, mixed with charcoal, and returned to the furnace. Heating progressed until the mass was molten. The cupric oxide would lose its oxygen by combustion with the carbon. When this stage of the process was judged to be complete, when as much of the copper oxide as possible had been reduced to metallic copper, the molten metal was 'poled'. The copper was stirred with fresh sticks of a green wood, usually hazel or chestnut, which caused agitation as vapour and gases were generated by the wood. This is a complex and curious process whose full function was not truly understood by those who did it.

Now the copper could be run into the forehearth as before and allowed to chill, often by dousing with water. The first disk lifted off the surface, and perhaps the second, usually contained slags, so these were set aside for remelting in the next furnace run. Successive disks were chilled with water, pried up and lifted off with tongs, and quenched in a nearby tub (Fig. 17). These disks were known as rosette copper, on account of their shape and colour, and were of remarkable purity. A purity of better than 98 per cent was often achieved, which is quite a tribute to the skill and expertise of the furnace operators, although it took several furnace runs at each stage to achieve this kind of quality.

Copper smelting techniques varied considerably from region to region so the above description is necessarily brief and lacking in specific details. Developments during the century and more following the major publications cited earlier tended rather to streamline production than to innovate technically.

Rosette copper, as well as ingots and plate, were exported all over Europe for local processing and further working. Because it required a good deal more calamine by volume than copper to make brass, the copper was often transported to a site close to the source of calamine. However, Nuremberg's position on one of the major trade routes, and the requirements of its craftsmen for large quantities of finished brass, made production within the city or its environs economically feasible.

CEMENTATION

The process of producing brass from copper and a zinc ore is known rather loosely as cementation. Calamine, anhydrous zinc carbonate ($ZnCO_3$), was the chief ore used for this from prehistoric times until the nineteenth century, although around the year 1550 Erasmus Ebner used the accretions of zinc oxide from furnaces used for refining Rammelsberg lead ores (cited in Ercker, 254 n.). He calls this substance *Ofenbruch*; it was also known in England as tutty. Lazarus Ercker, writing a quarter of a century later, states that several brass works in his time were using *Ofengalmei*, or furnace calamine, from Goslar (p. 254). This development was doubtless very

FIG. 17. The refining of copper from *De Re Metallica*. The metal which runs into the forehearth is chilled with water and disks of rosette copper are lifted off and quenched in a tub

profitable as tutty was previously regarded as a waste product and discarded. There was probably an accumulation of centuries of it around all lead works waiting to be used. Nevertheless, the calamine process continued as the chief source of brass (apart from recycling) even after it became possible in the mid-eighteenth century to produce alloys directly from the two metals. Some of the continuing popularity of calamine brass may have been due to its working characteristics. Ercker states that brass from Goslar (i.e. that made from furnace calamine, or tutty) gives 'a gray-ish fracture, and one has to be careful in annealing so that the metal will not crack on working' (p. 257). As this 'calamine' came from lead smelting furnaces it would contain a fairly high proportion of lead. Rapid cooling of the brass would give an even distribution of lead globules and a greyish colour on breaking. The resulting brass would be very fine for casting, as leaded brasses tend to have good flow char-acteristics, but it would be less tractable in cold working.

Cementation relies upon the property of zinc that at temperatures of around 850°C its equilibrium vapour pressure over calamine is above that of zinc over brass. Thus, when zinc is reduced from an oxidized state in the presence of copper, the zinc vapour will diffuse readily into the solid copper and the reaction may pro-ceed to completion. The theoretical upper limit to zinc diffusion into copper dur-ing cementation is in the order of 30 per cent (Craddock, 9–10);[8] no early brasses have zinc contents in excess of the low thirties and most are much lower. The rate of zinc uptake is proportional to the temperature and the surface area of the copper. If it is merely 'beaten small' (*klein geschlagen*) (Weigel, p. 315) the surface area will be much less than if very finely granulated.

Preparation of calamine for cementation was often a two-stage process where the mineral was first calcined by roasting at an intermediate temperature to convert it to zinc oxide:

$$ZnCO_3 = ZnO + CO_2 \text{ (gas)}.$$

The zinc oxide so produced was then mixed with finely divided charcoal and such fluxes as salt, alum, or urine in crucibles. The broken copper was laid on top, fol-lowed sometimes by a layer of crushed glass which would prevent loss of zinc through evaporation. On heating a reduction reaction would take place producing metallic zinc and carbon monoxide:

$$ZnO + C = Zn + CO \text{ (gas)}.$$

Once the process was judged complete, the heat of the furnace would be in-creased to melt the brass. An iron tool was inserted and stirred in the liquid metal

[8] Craddock provides a synopsis of metallurgical work by Werner and Haedeke on defining an upper limit for zinc concentration during cementation.

to test the melt. Occasionally the brass was returned to the furnace and remelted, although Ercker sees no virtue in this (see below).

An interesting text in the study of the metal used by the Nuremberg musical-instrument industry is that of Christoph Weigel, who describes the calamine process in the *Abbildung. . .* of 1698 mentioned previously. Although the passage describing the work of the *Messingbrenner* (pp. 313–16) gives an apparently credible picture of work which perhaps took place in Nuremberg at his time of writing, its originality is questionable. In fact, in all but a few particulars, this passage is an exact paraphrase of Ercker's of over a century earlier. Ercker's description of the process is worth recording in full:

When they wish to make brass, they will have round furnaces built underground, in which the draft can urge the fire through holes in the lower part of the furnace. Into one of these furnaces they charge eight pots or crucibles at once, let them get warm and then hot, and, when they are hot, lift them out quickly and charge the calamine. They have a special elongated scoop which is also a measuring device, so that they know how much they are using and so that they can divide about 46 pounds of calamine among the eight pots. After this is done, they put eight pounds of copper, broken into small pieces, on top of the calamine in each pot and replace the pots. They expose them to a lively fire for nine hours, during which nine hours they use up one and a half baskets of charcoal. When this charcoal has burned down for the afore-mentioned number of hours, they use an iron tool to feel around in the matter in the pots to see how it has melted; then they keep it molten for another good hour, so that it will graduate. Subsequently they remove the pots from the furnace, and, if they wish to have cakes of brass, they pour the contents of all eight pots into a round hole in the ground, and, while the matter is still hot, they break the cakes into pieces. However, they leave the pieces close together, which gives the brass a beautiful yellow color in its fracture . . . Some brass melters return the brass again to the furnace, especially if they wish to give it a higher color; but there is no gain or profit in such a procedure, since the expense exceeds the advantage. (p. 256)[9]

You should know, further, that brass undergoes an increase in weight when it is made. When you put into the pots 46 pounds [of calamine and 64 pounds*] of copper, the weight of the brass is increased by 26 pounds in nine hours, so that 90 pounds of brass are always poured (p. 257)[10]

The major difference between Ercker's work and the paraphrase by Weigel is in the weight of calamine specified. Ercker recommends 46 pounds of calamine to 64 pounds of copper and states that the copper increases in weight by 26 pounds during cementation. Ignoring for simplicity the slight difference in atomic weights of copper and zinc (63.5 and 65.4 respectively), this gives a brass with approximately

---

[9] This and the following quotation are from Sisco and Smith's translation.

[10] The interpolation marked with an asterisk by the translators adjusts the text to agree with the earlier paragraph.

29 per cent zinc which is an excellent yield. Weigel, on the other hand, recommends 68 pounds of calamine be added to the same weight of copper although, because this is near the upper limit of zinc concentration by cementation anyway, the brass will be only slightly richer in zinc. One might conclude that either Weigel has transcribed the information incorrectly, or the calamine was of much poorer quality. However, throughout his treatise Ercker is probably discussing the use of furnace calamine, which is zinc oxide. Weigel, on the other hand, is referring to naturally occurring calamine, zinc carbonate, which Nuremberg brass founders apparently used almost exclusively (Hachenberg, 11).[11] Assuming, then, that the natural calamine was not first roasted to convert it to zinc oxide, the difference in molecular weights (125.5 and 81.5 respectively) agrees quite closely with the difference in weight of calamine specified by the two authors. (If Weigel is, indeed, describing the production of brass from natural calamine it seems unnecessary to allow the broken pieces of brass cake to lie close to each other while cooling. This is more likely to be necessary if the brass contains considerable quantities of lead.)

Ercker provides an illustration of the furnace and ancilliary equipment, but he obviously requires the reader to have a healthy imagination (Fig. 18). The lid of the under-floor furnace is clearly visible at the top left (B), but the arrangement of eight crucibles, to be charged from the larger, upside-down master crucible (A), must be visualized as being situated below floor level, beneath the lid. Perhaps this is what the dotted line around the group is meant to convey. To further confuse the picture, the handles of the tongs for carrying the small crucibles have been shoved quite artistically into the mouth of the master crucible. Ercker and the publisher's *Formschneider* appear to have lacked a close working relationship.

Both Weigel and Ercker agree on nine hours for cementation to reach completion, but this is actually a very short length of time. In general others recommend at least twelve hours and often much longer. Although Biringuccio states that at least twenty-four hours are necessary, which confirms the reports of other authors, his description of the process is unreliable at best.

There were actually *two* brass industries in Nuremberg and it is important to differentiate between them; the production of brass from copper and calamine described above was the smaller industry. A larger casting industry produced the so-called *Nürnberger Tand*—a wide range of cast articles. The latter industry had its workshops within the city and thrived upon scrap metal. It was a common practice to use scrap brass, or *Schrott*, and old household articles and other artefacts were in great demand by the brass smelters. (Haedeke, p. 30) The casting industry which

---

[11] Both Helmut Ullwer and Karl Hachenberg provide excellent overviews of the material used by brass instrument makers, including discussions of the structure and the physical and chemical properties of the alloy (see Bibliography).

FIG. 18. Lazarus Ercker's illustration of the furnace for cementation of brass. The lid of the underfloor furnace is seen in (B) but the eight crucibles must be visualized below floor level. The carrying tongs for the crucibles (A) are shown inserted into the master crucible (H). Note the angled Breton (or British) stones on the right for casting sheet brass (G)

produced such items as candlesticks, figurines and bowls did not produce sheet brass or wire. Nevertheless, even the brass producers who used the calamine process often added scrap brass to the melt, but not in great quantities.

PRODUCTION OF BRASS STOCK

Once brass had been made in the furnace it was either poured into moulds and broken up for further processing, poured into ingots, or cooled between flat limestone slabs to produce sheet and bar stock. Ercker describes the latter:

If they wish to make kettles or other hammered ware out of the brass, they cast the contents of the pots (crucibles) into large plates by pouring the brass between large stones that are specially made for the purpose, which are called British stones (*Britannische Steine*) (after the place whence they are imported). From these plates they can later cut stock for drawing into wire or hammering into whatever form they wish. (p. 256)

The *Britannische Steine* have been translated variously as Breton stones or British stones. Although their exact source is not specified, it is clear that they must have been selected for their ability to accept a smooth surface finish, and for an extremely low coefficient of expansion, and thus a low probability of spalling or cracking under the thermal shock of receiving molten metal. These slabs of stone can be seen in Ercker's illustration (see Fig. 18). They are angled, presumably to make pouring more convenient, and must have been grouted with lute (a fine clay used in furnaces) to prevent leakage. Galon's illustration of them shows no major difference, except in scale, while Diderot shows the stones laid more conveniently in a horizontal plane.

Brass sheet cast between stones was by no means consistent in quality, nor did the craftsmen necessarily demand the best. During examination of an astrolabe made in 1537 by Georg Hartman, one of the most respected makers of navigational instruments of his day, defects were found on the inner surfaces which led the metallurgist to conclude that '. . . surface defects were sufficiently common in the brass available to the instrument-maker that he could not afford to reject an entire sheet because of their presence' (Gordon, 95). Gordon also states that 'It should be kept in mind that pouring ingots of the quality required for making brass sheet with a good surface finish remained a problem for brass makers up through the first part of the present century' (p. 96).

The cast sheets were then sent to be sawn into suitable sizes:

The brass is then in the form of great flat blocks or sheets, and these are afterwards cut by a brass cutter or sawyer into bars, staves or ingots of one, two or it may be three fingers' breadth. They employ a machine for this purpose which is like that used for wood in the saw-mills (Haedeke, 29–30).[12]

---

[12] This is Haedeke's translation of the passage from Weigel's *Messingbrenner*.

FIG. 19. Christoph Weigel's illustration of the *Messingschlager*, or brass beater, working with a water-powered trip hammer. Because the hammer head is distinctly rectangular, the brass tends to be elongated into a strip while only gaining a little in width

The saw used for slitting the brass into strips was probably a water-powered pit saw, doubtless lubricated and cooled by a constant flow of water. Perhaps the sawyers also found a way of recovering the swarf by allowing the run-off to pass into a settling tank.

Bars of brass which were 'one, two or three fingers wide', and as thick as the cast sheet, would be passed along to the *Messingschlager* to be beaten into strips or plates (Fig. 19). There is a thorough, but rather late, description of this and other brass-making processes in *Vollständige theoretische und praktische Geschichte der Erfindungen* by J. J. Flick of 1798 (pp. 182–220), although what he has to say about trumpet-making itself is not very useful.

It has been pointed out that one of the chief differences between old brass and the modern material is the orientation of the crystal structure, and the consequent measurable and perceptible differences in acoustic response. (Gug, 16–19) Modern brass is passed through a rolling mill which makes it thinner and increases its length, but alters its width hardly at all. When examined under the microscope a distinct longitudinal orientation is observed in the structure. With hammering, it has been pointed out, the metal tends to be spread in all directions and therefore does not have this longitudinal orientation. The true situation is not quite so clear-cut; if the *Messingschlager* were using a hammer with a square face then the brass block would certainly expand evenly in all directions (except, of course, thickness!). In the illustration by Weigel this is clearly not the case; the hammer head is distinctly rectangular. There will therefore be more expansion in a direction at right angles to the broad side, and less at $90°$ from this. The ratio of expansion in these two directions will be the same as the ratio of the lengths of the hammer head sides. Thus, even in hammered brass there will be a distinct longitudinal orientation. For organ reeds these considerations may be very important, but in the case of brass instruments any orientation is likely to be destroyed in annealing of the metal after working.

Excessive hammering work-hardens brass, causing it to become brittle. To avoid cracking, the metal must be annealed by heating at frequent intervals to make it malleable. This is an expensive and time-consuming process and it is reasonable to assume that attempts would be made to supply the brass beater with as thin a cast sheet as possible. No accurate method of measuring thickness existed in the brass works; thickness of the metal was not measured directly. Instead, a given weight of brass was hammered out into strips of a certain length. It was apparently designated in 'folds'—the greater the number of folds, the thinner the sheet.[13]

As mentioned previously, the quality of cast and hammered sheet was not always of the best. It was examined and graded and only the pieces with few flaws were passed along to the final craftsman, the *Messingschaber*, or Brass Scraper, shown in Weigel's illustration (Fig. 20). It was his job to remove the black mill scale from one side. This presented the user with a clean surface on which to begin work, and also enabled identification of substandard pieces.

The use of a rolling mill in the seventeenth and eighteenth centuries for the finishing of brass sheet should not be discounted. It is known that a rolling mill was in use in Nuremberg in 1550 for the goldsmith's trade (Lietzmann *et al.*, 245). Its potential for making sheets of other materials must have been recognized fairly early, but perhaps for Guild reasons it was not used in large-scale production until much later. It has been argued that the machinists of the time could not have produced rollers of sufficient accuracy, but if the mandrels upon which trumpets and

---

[13] Gug's description (p. 48) of the preparation of thin brass for organ reeds is equally valid for the material supplied to the trumpet-maker.

Fɪɢ. 20. Christoph Weigel's illustration of the *Messingschaber*, or brass scraper, removing the scale from sheets so as to prepare them for use and to allow the purchaser to judge their quality

trombones were made are any indication, the machining skills certainly did exist.

Finally, after an intricate series of chemical and physical operations, the metal was ready for use. Our reliance on modern manufacturing techniques often causes us to forget that all the stages through which the metal passed were supervised by highly skilled craftsmen. The sheet brass purchased by the trumpet-maker was of exceptional thinness and consistency. He could, and probably did, hide surface defects on the inside of material rolled to make tubes, but the pieces from which bells were hammered would need to be flawless.

There is little information on the thickness of metal until late in the period when Johann Samuel Halle writes in *Werkstäte der heutigen Künste* of 1764 that the metal supplied to the trumpet-makers is 'of the eighth or ninth gauge number of sheet brass (*Latunmessings*), is 6 feet long, one and a half feet wide, and the thickness is the thickness of notepaper' (iii. 372).[14] Metal gauges were by this time becoming standardized but his mention of the thickness of note paper indicates a wish to give the reader a simple standard of comparison. Nevertheless, in his very large section on papermaking (i. 139 ff.) Halle makes no mention of thicknesses of paper, and no specific mention of notepaper. Modern notepaper is much thinner than the metal of the lightest trumpet.

From measurement of extant instruments it appears that the starting thickness varies between 0.70 mm. in some heavy instruments to about 0.40 mm. Apparently a range of thicknesses was offered depending upon the finished instrument's use or the preference of the player. J. E. Altenburg describes the different weights of finished instruments and the relationship of weight to tone in the various registers:

A trumpet of strong thick metal may be durable and useful for field-piece (*Feldstück*) and principale (*Principal*) playing; but in the high register towards the clarino (*Clarin*) it demands more wind, has an unpleasant sound, and therefore is altogether unsuitable for the clarino player (*Clarinist*) and concert trumpeter. However, if the metal is too thin and weak, it is true that [such a trumpet] can be played easily in the high register and has a [more] pleasant tone than [one of heavy metal]; but it is not strong and penetrating enough in the low register for field piece and principale playing, and not at all durable.

For common use, therefore, a medium kind of metal is the best. However, if another [person] should want to employ a stronger type for principale and a weaker type for clarino [playing], according to the nature of the part he has to play, he would not be incorrect. (p. 10)

Although his book was finally published at the close of the eighteenth century, we can be sure that Altenburg was harking back to an earlier era. The base thicknesses of the metal from a selection of extant instruments appear in Table 1.

Physical and Chemical Characteristics of Brass

In the mixing ratios resulting from cementation with calamine, brass exists as a solid solution of zinc in copper. As copper is in the largest proportion it is the solvent; the zinc is the solute. In the solid state copper and zinc atoms are distributed in a regular structure within the alloy. Some alloys exist as simple solutions at any temperature, no matter what the concentration of their constituents, because each is perfectly soluble in the other. Copper and nickel are examples of metals which form a so-called single-phase alloy. Although solubility of most metals is often high at elevated temperatures, in the majority of cases there is a limit to solid solubility. A

---

[14] *Man gebraucht dazu die achte oder neunte Nummer des Latunmessings, dessen Tafeln 6 Fus lang, anderhalb Fus weit, und die Dikke wie die Dikke des Notenpappiers ist.*

TABLE 1. *Metal thickness and overall diameter of tubing on the yards of eleven instruments*

Instrument	Date	Thickness (mm.)	Diameter (mm.)
Anton Schnitzer	1599	0.60	12.90
Sebastian Hainlein	1657	0.55	11.80
Paul Hainlein	1664	0.50	11.90
Wolff Birkholz	1680	0.45	11.80
Johann Wilhelm Haas	*c.*1700	0.60	11.80
Johann Leonhard Ehe II	early 18th	0.425	11.80
Johann Wilhelm Haas	mid 18th	0.50	12.00
Wolf Magnus Ehe	late 18th	0.50	12.00
Johann Wilhelm Haas	late 18th	0.50	11.00
Georg Friedrich Steinmetz	late 18th	0.60	11.70
Cornelius Steinmetz	*c.*1800	0.475	11.95

maximum of approximately 30 per cent zinc by weight will dissolve in copper at room temperature. If brass contains more than 30 per cent zinc, the excess zinc will precipitate out on cooling in a high zinc phase which also contains copper. This differential solubility, and varying proportions of the constituents, result in definable phases in the alloy. At a concentration above the solubility of zinc in copper the alloy will not be homogenous—there will be a phase of copper containing the maximum possible zinc, and there will be a second phase having a different compositional ratio and a different crystalline structure from the first. Brass is thus a polyphase alloy. This is best illustrated with a phase diagram where percentages of copper and zinc are plotted against temperature (Fig. 21). The single-phase alloys with 30 per cent or less of zinc, known as the alpha brasses, occupy the left, and mercifully less complicated, side of the phase diagram (*Metals Handbook*, 301). With most alloys one cannot refer strictly to a melting *point*; there is generally a melting *range*. The alloy begins to melt at a temperature called the solidus, and is fully melted at the liquidus temperature. The liquidus and solidus lines enclose the slender triangle shown on the phase diagram between the solid and liquid phases. (Occasionally the term 'melting point' is applied to the onset of solidus, while the onset of liquidus is called the 'flow point'.)

MICROSTRUCTURE

On the primary level the atoms of metals stack themselves in one of several regular, geometrical lattice formations, which gives metal its characteristic crystalline structure. Copper possesses a face-centred cubic crystal structure (Fig. 22). When solid solution takes place (i.e. when one metal is dissolved completely in the other) the atoms of the solute must be introduced intimately into this lattice. The two kinds

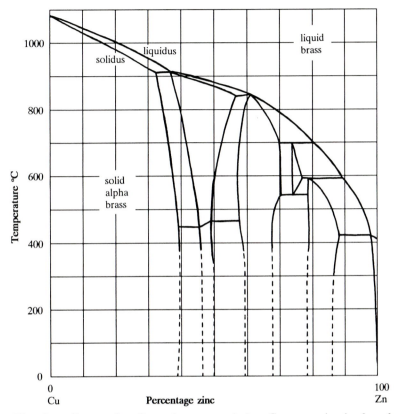

FIG. 21. The phase diagram for alloys of copper and zinc. Concentration is plotted against temperature. Alloys with low concentrations of zinc in copper, known as the alpha brasses, occupy the left side of the diagram. The solidus and liquidus of the alpha brasses are shown. (Based on *Metals Handbook*)

of solid solution are substitutional and interstitial, the type depending upon the relative size of the solvent and solute atoms. For example, if the solute atoms are very small compared with those of the solvent, they may occupy interstitial spaces within the existing lattice; they may distort, expand, or contract the lattice, but not rearrange it. Because atoms of copper and zinc are similar in size, brass is a substitutional solid solution. A space in the lattice normally occupied by a copper atom will be occupied instead by a zinc atom (see Fig. 22). The position of the zinc atoms in the lattice is random. Zinc and copper atoms differ slightly in size (Zn 1.33Å, Cu 1.28Å) and the presence of the zinc atoms therefore causes strain in the lattice. This strain or distortion is the feature which provides a limit to solid solubility at low temperatures, except in cases where the constituent atoms are very close in dimen-

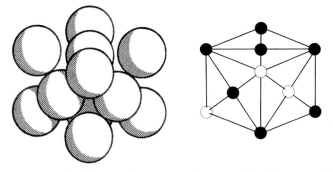

FIG. 22. The face-centred cubic crystal structure of copper. The diagram on the right shows alpha brass where random substitution of zinc atoms (white) occurs within the lattice of copper atoms (black)

sions (Carter, 207–12). The single-phase alloy of copper and nickel mentioned above is an example of the latter class.

On the secondary level, an alloy exhibits a grain structure. As it cools and solidifies it begins to crystallize. Crystals begin forming and meet each other to produce grains which give brass its characteristic granular texture (Fig. 23). Each grain has a precise crystal orientation based upon the lattice structure, but the individual grains bear a random relationship to each other in orientation. The interfaces of these grains are known as grain boundaries.

Unlike such ionic crystalline structures as salt, metals have the ability to deform plastically; the atoms of the metal can slip over one another causing deformation of the microstructure, rather than breaking. Slipping takes place in specific planes of atoms which are oriented to the lattice structure. This planar slipping takes the form of dislocation lines. Paradoxically, the energy required to initiate slipping is not sufficient to allow it to continue. The energy required to propagate an existing slip, or to start one on a new plane, increases as the metal is already strained. This feature gives brass its characteristic work-hardening properties.[15] The motion of a dislocation line is further inhibited in brasses by large impurities. 'Locking' of the atom planes due to dissimilar sized atoms prevents slippage.

Microscopic examination of brass before and after cold working shows the effect of stress upon the grains (Fig. 24). Rapid cooling of a hot, disordered alloy results in a fine polycrystalline structure, and a consequently soft and easily deformed metal. Rapid cooling was found to be essential when working with early brasses because only under these conditions do the impurities tend to remain in solution.

---

[15] B. A. Rogers gives excellent basic descriptions of the properties of alloys.

FIG. 23. Photomicrograph at 300× of the grain texture of 70% copper, 30% zinc brass. (Annealed at 350°C for 20 min. and water quenched; etched with ammonia and hydrogen peroxide.) (Photo courtesy of Buehler Ltd.)

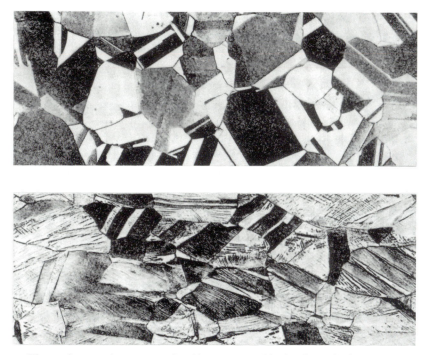

FIG. 24. Photomicrograph at 300× of 70% copper, 30% zinc brass before (top) and after (bottom) cold working. These samples show a cross-section of the rolling direction; i.e. a side view of the longitudinal axis. The sample in the lower illustration has been reduced 25% by rolling and the grains are elongated and distorted in the direction of working. (Annealed at 400°C for 10 min. and water quenched; etched with ammonia and hydrogen peroxide.) (Photo courtesy of Buehler Ltd.)

Slow cooling (as noted in the section on cementation) causes the impurities to precipitate out, producing a less tractable metal. Working a soft, fine-grained brass by hammering, drawing, burnishing, etc. causes elongation of the grains in the direction of working and a progressive increase in the energy required to deform the metal further. The trumpet-maker aimed to leave all parts of the finished instrument in a relatively hard condition by cold working them in the final stages of construction.

CORROSION

Metals rarely exist in nature in the pure state—they are most often found oxidized in the form of ores. Oxidation lowers the free energy of a chemical system, allowing the metal to occupy a more stable state. A characteristic of metals is the freeness of their constituent electrons. When metal atoms are stacked in a regular, undisturbed lattice each atom shares its electrons with each adjacent atom and a state of equilibrium exists. In fact, one cannot say that a certain electron belongs to a certain atom; the atoms can be better likened to discrete nuclei surrounded by a cloud of shared electrons. It is this property which gives metals their facility to conduct electricity and heat. The surface of the metal quite clearly features atoms whose electrons are unshared and the metal is therefore in a high energy state at its surface, or at discontinuities and impurities in its grain structure, and will react as an electron donor with any element which has a deficit of electrons. Oxygen, sulphur and oxides of sulphur and nitrogen are some typical electron recipients. Their interaction with the metal atoms provides mutual satisfaction.

Oxidation of a metal occurs during corrosion. Copper and zinc can form oxides, sulphides, sulphates, nitrates and so on, depending upon the conditions under which they corrode. Corrosion brings the components of a chemical reaction to a lower energy level with a consequent loss of energy by the system. Reduction is the opposite. It requires an input of energy and leaves the metal in a higher energy state. Removing oxides and sulphides from metals during smelting is an obvious example of a reduction reaction.

In stable atmospheric conditions some metals form a uniform, stable oxidation layer called a passivating layer. Each of the surface atoms reacts with an oxidizing agent to produce a stable chemical system with low free energy. This layer prevents access of other oxidizers, resulting in an equilibrium between the metal and its environment. The passivating layer which forms in ordinary atmospheric conditions gives old brass its characteristic patination. This layer is never microscopically complete because of disruptions at grain boundaries and impurities. The differing energy states between components of alloys can cause small galvanic cells to be formed in the presence of salts and water. Copper and zinc will react with each other under these conditions. This action usually takes place at discontinuities in the alloy, such

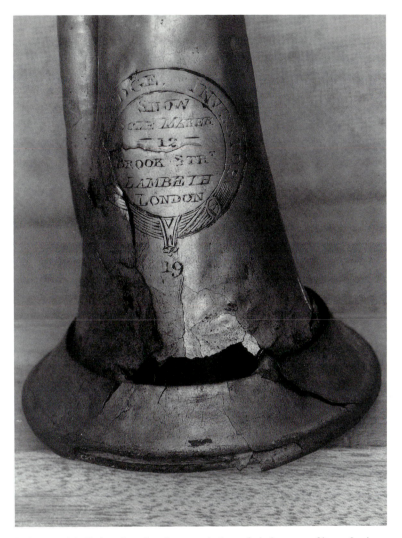

FIG. 25. A damaged bell showing the characteristic embrittlement of brass by intergranular corrosion. This is sometimes known as 'season cracking'. It can be caused by attack by acids or ammonia. (Bugle by Snow of London, Bate Collection, University of Oxford, No. 70)

as grain boundaries, where it results in so-called intergranular corrosion. This gives old brass a crazed appearance and in extreme cases may result in total disintegration.

Intergranular corrosion is prevalent in brass which has been hardened and stressed by cold working. Hardening introduces strain and distortion to the grains, giving a far higher potential for oxidative degradation. It was the aim of the trumpet-maker to leave the bell of an instrument as hard as possible for mechanical, and perhaps also acoustical reasons. When an old trumpet bell becomes damaged its brittleness causes it to crumple and split (Fig. 25). The type of corrosion affecting cold worked brass is often called stress corrosion, although it occurs at the grain boundaries and is quite often precipitated by corrosive agents such as ammonia which have come in contact with the metal from its environment.

In view of both the susceptibility of old brass to intergranular corrosion, and the attractive and stable passivating layer which forms on it, polishing is rarely beneficial. Clean, stable brass is best stored in an environment with a low relative humidity and free of atmospheric pollutants. When clean brass is handled, gloves should be worn.

EXAMINATION OF TRUMPET BRASSES

Although attempts over the last decade or so to recreate old brasses for the use of modern trumpet-makers indicate the importance of authenticity to both the craftsman and the musician, this reintroduction of early technology has led to some misconceptions. Firstly, it is often supposed, erroneously, that brass bars must be hammered out into thin strips in the way described by Weigel in order to give the grains of the metal the correct longitudinal orientation. Modern-day hammer mills have even been constructed in order to pursue this. That the orientation is a factor in influencing the acoustic properties of the metal is beyond dispute.[16] However, as the brass of the bell, bows, and yards is heated close to red heat during soldering, and the bell reheated several times during annealing and working, it is clear that any grain orientation formed in the production of the brass will be lost and re-formed several times over. The final orientation of the grains *does not* result from the production of the sheet metal, but from the forming of the parts during the making of the musical instrument.

A second misconception is that brass made by cementation with calamine is somehow different from brass made by direct alloying. Manufacturers of brass instruments have advertised their use of 'calamine brass', causing the unwary to assume that it is a different alloy. It was discovered in the late eighteenth century that this was not so; that the two were one and the same. In both cases the metal is a solid solution of zinc in copper. One important difference between modern alpha brass (usually an alloy of 70–30 copper–zinc, called cartridge brass) and its earlier counterpart is in the purity of the ingredients. The presence of inclusions like iron and copper sulphides and globules of lead in early brasses may have some influence on the acoustics, but this has yet to be proven.

---

[16] See, for example, Gug's experimental work on the brass used for organ reeds.

TABLE 2. *Analyses of two Nuremberg trumpets and three Viennese trumpets*

Instrument	Date	Percentage of constituent metals							
		Cu	Zn	Sn	Pb	Fe	Ni	Ag	Sb
P. Hainlein	1664	76.99	22.02	<0.20	0.17	0.19	0.32	0.16	0.03
J. L. Ehe II	c.1700	78.74	20.35	<0.20	0.12	0.21	0.25	0.08	<0.01
A. Kerner (father)	1769	74.32	20.35	<0.20	1.17	0.09	0.08	0.08	0.07
A. Kerner (son)	1793	69.09	30.26	<0.20	0.21	0.20	0.07	0.17	<0.01
I. Kerner	1793	71.52	28.13	<0.20	0.12	0.11	0.07	0.05	<0.01

Notes: Note the differences in the alloys of the instruments by the two younger Kerners: instruments which were made in the same workshop and are dated the same year. In order to avoid possible inaccuracy due to low content of zinc on the surface of the brass, the samples from these instruments were taken by deep scraping within the bell on the side opposite the seam. (These figures by kind permission of the Trompetenmuseum Bad Säckingen, Karl Hachenberg, and a private collection in West Germany.)

The chief area in which authenticity in the use of metal might be assured is in the percentage of zinc which the brass contains. Over hundreds of years of brass production in Nuremberg (and elsewhere) zinc concentration tended on the whole to increase to a maximum of around 30 per cent. Some typical analyses of dated brass instruments are shown in Table 2. An extremely useful study on the analysis of Nuremberg jetons (brass trading counters) traces their production in an unbroken line from c.1475 to 1888 (Mitchiner et al., 114–55). If we assume that the brass used in the striking of jetons was of the same stock as that used by other craftsmen, we have a full chronology of Nuremberg brass compositions. It is apparent from this study that zinc concentration varied quite widely between makers and dates. This may be due to differing batches of metal, variations in the yield of zinc from calamine (several grades were available), or the choice of the individual craftsman from a range offered by the foundry. It is known that some jeton-makers favoured certain qualities of stock brass, and that a low zinc brass was also available (Mitchiner et al., 137) (probably made by melting brass with extra copper, rather than through low-yield cementation). But did the instrument-makers choose from a substantially different stock from other craftsmen and did they have preferences based upon such factors as colour, working characteristics, and even price? Wide variations of the copper–zinc ratio are seen in the analyses of instruments in Table 2, and it is apparent from these and other analyses that no pattern emerges. The zinc content of the two trumpets by the Kerner brothers shows that even in the same years, and from the same workshop, stock brass varied considerably. The absence of a systematic study of brass instruments makes conclusions difficult to draw, but it is certain that alloys of between 20 and 25 per cent zinc were the norm for seventeenth- and eighteenth-century trumpets.

Silver

Although brass was by far the most common metal for trumpets and trombones, silver was used for ceremonial or especially decorative instruments. The great majority of silver instruments in modern collections are trumpets, although according to Christoph Weigel silver was also used for trombones on special occasions: 'His Highness has recently commissioned for the Royal Orchestra a silver trombone from Nuremberg for Europe's most famous trombonist, Hellwig'[17] (Weigel, 233). How would such an instrument perform? Silver instruments tend to be made heavier in construction than brass ones because, even when alloyed with copper, silver is softer than brass. An instrument, or any other work of art, would be ordered and paid for by the total weight of silver used in its construction. No doubt, use of the precious metal for its monetary value compromised musical performance to a certain extent. J. E. Altenburg states that 'the opinion that these [silver] are superior in sound to those of brass is unfounded. Rather the contrary is proven by experience' (pp. 9–10).

Production of Silver

Silver is occasionally found native in fragments big enough to be separated from the worthless rock mechanically and treated separately. However, most silver production in Europe during the Middle Ages and Renaissance was associated with the smelting of other metals, particularly lead and to a lesser extent copper. Once the rich mines in the New World were discovered and opened to exploitation in the seventeenth century, importation of silver occupied a major place (Tylecote, *History of Metallurgy*, 97). Until then local production during smelting of lead and copper produced silver as a profitable by-product.

SILVER FROM COPPER ORES

If the yield of silver was considered economical, locally mined lead ore was sometimes added to the furnace charge of copper ore, or extra lead was melted into the forehearth prior to releasing the charge. As silver and lead are both almost totally insoluble in copper at low temperatures, the trace of silver is preferentially dissolved in the lead, which forms a separate phase from the copper. The resulting lead–copper–silver cake lifted from the forehearth was treated by liquation to melt the lead–silver alloy away from the copper. Agricola illustrates a liquation furnace (Fig. 26) where the large cakes of *Werck* are placed on edge on a slightly sloping trough

---

[17] *ihren Hoff-Musicum und dazumahl berühmtesten Trombonisten in Europa | Nahmens Hellwig | mit einer zu Nürnberg verfertigten silbernen Posaunen allergnädigt beschencket.*

FIG. 26. A liquation furnace illustrated by Agricola. The round cakes of *Werck* are placed over the fire and the lead, with silver and other metals, is melted out, leaving a 'skeleton' consisting mostly of copper

and surrounded by firewood or charcoal enclosed with iron plates. As the lead–silver alloy required only a low temperature to melt, wood firing and an open construction were often quite adequate. On firing, the lead–silver dripped out of the cake and ran into the forehearth where it solidified, leaving behind a skeleton of the copper, which has a higher melting point, in the furnace. It was necessary to maintain a reducing atmosphere (excluding oxygen) during liquation by covering the lead thoroughly with hot coals, otherwise the lead would become oxidized. A constant temperature was also maintained. The exhausted liquation cakes, which contained a considerable amount of copper, were returned to the copper smelter, while the lead cake was further processed by cupellation, as detailed below.

SILVER FROM LEAD ORES

Most of the silver produced between the sixteenth and eighteenth centuries in Germany was a by-product of lead smelting. Provided the lead contained a minimum of some 300 to 400 g. of silver per tonne it was considered worth extracting (Tylecote, *History of Metallurgy*, 101). The most common ore of lead is the sulphide, galena (PbS), which often contains traces of argentite, the sulphide of silver. Agricola describes a furnace for smelting lead which differs hardly at all from the ones he used for copper. During smelting the spigot was left open and the lead ran into the forehearth as it was produced. The lead sulphide ore was reduced to metallic lead with the evolution of sulphur dioxide:

$$PbS + O_2 \text{ (gas)} = Pb + SO_2 \text{ (gas)}.$$

The trace of silver sulphide in the ore followed the same reaction. An earlier and much simpler process relied upon a double decomposition reaction; lead oxide (litharge) was first produced by partial roasting of the ore at a fairly low temperature:

$$2PbS + 3O_2 \text{ (gas)} = 2PbO + 2SO_2 \text{ (gas)}.$$

The lead oxide produced from this reaction then reacted with the remaining lead sulphide to give metallic lead and sulphur dioxide:

$$2PbO + PbS = 3Pb + SO_2 \text{ (gas)}.$$

In the earliest and crudest form of lead smelting both these reactions took place at the same time, although the yield was extremely low (Tylecote, *History of Metallurgy*, 97). The double decomposition reaction could be partially utilized in the blast-furnace by including the litharge produced from cupellation (see below) with the charge of ore.

CUPELLATION

Cupellation was practised on a fairly large scale at Rammelsberg in the Harz Mountains for the retrieval of silver during the smelting of lead ores. The cupellation furnace consisted of a cup-shaped hearth lined with bone ash and enclosed by a brick dome. In front was an aperture for raking the ore, and in the rear the tuyère connected to water- or hand-powered bellows. The process relies on the fact that lead and metallic and non-metallic impurities are a great deal easier to oxidize than silver. The lead cake was melted in the cupel and then further heated to between 900 and 1,000°C. A blast of air was directed across it, converting the lead to lead oxide, or litharge, which was periodically skimmed off the surface or allowed to flow out. Litharge also fluxed and dissolved those oxides which had not been absorbed into the bone ash bed. An additional fluxing agent may have been needed if tin or zinc were present. Heating and skimming continued until samples of the lead removed from the pool showed white spots which indicated that the cupellation was nearly complete. Soon a bead of relatively pure silver remained in the cupel. The silver was by no means purified after a single cupellation; the process would be repeated several times in a smaller cupel with the addition of granulated lead or copper. The completion of refining was assessed by dipping an iron bar into the molten silver and detaching the beads of metal which adhered. These were hammered flat, providing an elegant test of the purity of the silver by its ductility (Agricola, *De Re Metallica*, 487). Once cooled the plano-convex ingot of silver was hammered free of its adhering ash and scrubbed with brass wires (Fig. 27). Finally:

the Royal Inspector in the employment of the King or Prince, or the owner, lays the silver on a block of wood, and with an engraver's chisel he cuts out two small pieces, one from the under and the other from the upper side. These are tested by fire, in order to ascertain whether the silver is thoroughly refined or not, and at what price it should be sold to the merchants. Finally he impresses upon it the seal of the King or the Prince or the owner, and, near the same, the amount of the weight (Agricola, *De Re Metallica*, 489)

Production of Silver Stock

The mechanical procedures for producing silver stock were very similar to those used for brass. Casting, hammering, scraping, and possibly rolling were all equally applicable. Generally speaking, pure silver was considered too soft to be of much use for functional objects. It is an extremely malleable metal, second only to gold, and was therefore alloyed with copper to give it desirable working properties. The addition of up to 10 per cent copper prior to casting ingots provided a metal stock which could be shaped and finished with the same facility as brass.

FIG. 27. The preparation of silver illustrated by Agricola. Hemispherical ingots of silver are lifted out of the furnace, scrubbed with wire brushes and inscribed with the proof marks

Because silver is a precious metal it was necessary to establish a system of control in order to minimize the possibility of deception. The amount of copper alloyed with silver was strictly controlled. This has resulted in such well-established standards as sterling silver (7.5 per cent copper) and coin silver (10 per cent copper). The grades of silver in use in Germany were *fein* and *probe*. J. E. Altenburg speaks of Augsburg silver which was of particularly good quality (p. 9).

Physical and Chemical Characteristics of Silver

At low temperatures silver and copper are mutually insoluble except in very small quantities. They exist together in their alloy as separate (discrete) phases. Silver with a small percentage of copper is actually in two phases: a matrix of silver containing small amounts of dissolved copper surrounding inclusions of copper with small amounts of dissolved silver. This structure is visible under the microscope in prepared samples (Fig. 28). The phase diagram in Fig. 29 illustrates this feature of silver–copper alloys; the alpha silver zone at the far left, where a single-phase alloy exists, diminishes virtually to zero at room temperature.

Various properties of silver–copper alloys can be obtained by specific regimens of heating and cooling. If a silver-rich solid solution is quenched rapidly in water the copper, which would form the second phase on slow cooling, will remain in solution giving a soft, ductile alloy which is ideal for mechanical shaping. A soft alloy can also be produced by a very gradual decrease of temperature in a controlled furnace (McDonald *et al.*, 248–54). Working of the alloy by bending, hammering, burnishing, and so on soon causes work-hardening where a network of precipitated copper prevents smooth dislocation of the structure. This is the common finished state of silver artefacts.

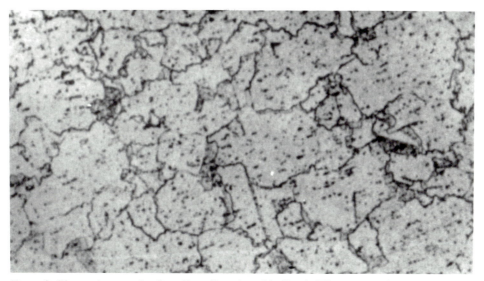

FIG. 28. Photomicrograph of sterling silver (92.5% silver). The copper phase appears uniformly and finely dispersed. Annealed and electrolytically lap polished; etched in chromosulphuric acid; magnification 300×. (Allison Butts and Charles D. Cox (eds.), *Silver: Economics, Metallurgy, and Use*, 1975 edition. Reprinted by permission of the Publisher 'All Rights Reserved')

The Metal

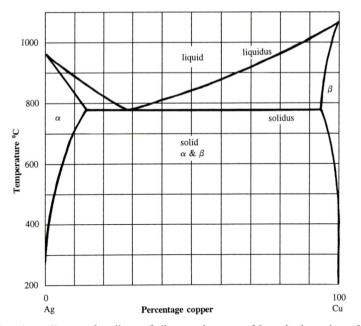

FIG. 29. The phase diagram for alloys of silver and copper. Note the lowering of the common melting point resulting from alloying. The lowest melting temperature is reached at the eutectic point (72% silver and 28% copper)

Corrosion

Silver reacts extremely slowly to oxygen but sulphur has a great affinity for it. The chief corrosion product of silver in a normal atmosphere is that caused by sulphur-bearing pollutants generally formed by the burning of fossil fuels. Silver tarnishes from a pale straw colour, through blue and brown, to a heavy black.

The alloying of copper with silver to enhance its mechanical properties results in a lowering of corrosion resistance. Since copper and silver exist as discrete phases in their alloy, the galvanic interaction between the two metals is more pronounced than in solution alloys. Because silver is 'nobler' than copper, being higher in the electrochemical series, it is protected from corrosion by the dissolution of copper. Copper will act as a 'sacrificial anode' while silver is 'cathodically protected'. In extreme cases, as in archaeological burials, copper artefacts have been totally lost while silver in close proximity has survived remarkably intact (Plenderleith and Werner, 193). Such extremes do not obtain in the normal environment of musical instruments, but green patches or spots caused by the preferential corrosion of copper in a silver alloy are not uncommon, especially where the metal has been repeatedly handled or cleaned with acidic mixtures or ammonia.

4

Solders and Fluxes

To make solder, of hammered and other kinds, which is necessary for so many artists and handworkers, and which to instrument-makers is indispensable, nothing in particular of great detail has been written. In many reports and writings one encounters usefulness and reliability are but sparingly found. The reason is easily guessed: many artists and handwork masters reckon to keep the secrets of soldering and hammersolders to themselves; they scarcely even declare them to their colleagues.

Johann Georg Friedrich Klein

The technique of joining metals with solder has its origins in prehistory. Archaeological objects of gold, silver, and bronze with intricately joined components indicate the early origins of the technique and the fine control possible. Soldering is based upon the ability of different metals to dissolve into each other by surface alloying. It is possible to heat one metal to its melting point and cause it to flow and dissolve into the surface of another metal which is still in the solid phase. Solders are often binary or ternary alloys; they are composed of two or three metals because alloying gives to the resultant material a number of useful properties.

The composition of solders can be adjusted so that they have a narrow but easily controllable temperature range over which they will melt and flow. A fairly wide range between solidus and liquidus will give a thick solder which flows slowly and can be used to fill gaps where two metal components cannot be brought into close contact. On the other hand, a tight join with virtually no space between components (like that used on the toothed bell seams of trumpets) can only be soldered with an alloy which quickly becomes fluid. In this case, solidus and liquidus are very close together and the melting range is therefore very narrow. If the flow range is too wide, and heating is slow, the constituent metals can separate out of the alloy. The fraction with the lower melting point may flow into the joint, leaving the metal which has a higher melting point on the surface. The flow range must also be below the melting point of the material to be joined, for obvious reasons, but not so low that surface alloying is compromised.[1]

The degree of wetting of the metal to be joined by the soldering alloy is an important consideration. As in fluids at room temperature, wetting of metals can be likened to surface tension; the surface tension must not be so high that the solder stays in beads on the joint as water will on a greasy surface. Wetting relies upon high free energy at the metal surface and this, in turn, depends upon the metals used in the solder. The addition of zinc, for example, to a soldering alloy results in greatly increased wetting.

A process of trial and error over many centuries has resulted in a useful range of alloys specifically tailored to their applications. Nowadays solders are broadly defined as hard or soft. The hard solders are usually taken to include all the alloys of copper, silver, and zinc, but these may also include small quantities of other metals like tin, cadmium, and nickel. Brazing materials, which are in effect high zinc brasses (sometimes ambiguously called spelters, a term which originally referred only to zinc), are included in this category. In making a hard-soldered joint the temperature of the metal is raised to red heat and diffusion of the solder into the surfaces gives an extremely strong join. There is no true dividing line between solder and substrate; they blend into one another. In contrast, soft solders are usually based upon lead and tin, but may also include bismuth, cadmium, and antimony. They are applied at much lower temperatures than hard solders and lack mechanical strength due to both their softness and their lack of penetration.

A slightly different emphasis on the types of solder was made in the eighteenth century and earlier, one based more upon the use to which the solder joint would be subjected. Johann Georg Friedrich Klein (1760) follows common practice in categorizing the solders as *schlag-* and *schnell-Lothen*, or 'hammerable' and 'quick' solders. The malleable, hard solder would be used in applications where further shaping of the metal was planned—the trumpet bell is the obvious example—while the quick, or soft, solder would be used for low-temperature, low-stress applications.

Nowadays soldering alloys are available from suppliers in the form of sheet, wire, granules, and so on, and soldering is done by applying the ready-made alloy directly to the work. This is a comparatively recent development, although Klein deals in some detail with the preparation of granular alloys. Almost all the early authors recommend that the individual components of the solder be ground together, mixed with the flux, and applied to the work as a mixture. Alloying only takes place upon heating during soldering.

[1] Herbert Maryon's book *Metalworking and Enamelling* provides a thorough discussion of the types of solder and their uses from antiquity to the present. This is, without doubt, the best treatise by a modern craftsman on traditional technique.

Solders for Brass

Solders used on brass instruments over the period under discussion fall into two convenient categories: the post-zinc and the pre-zinc solders, i.e. those where metallic zinc was added deliberately and the ones used before this. A fusible brass of relatively low melting point (now known as Muntz metal) can be made from 60 per cent copper and 40 per cent zinc. In the phase diagram for brass (see Fig. 21) a vertical line at 40 per cent zinc shows an alloy with a melting point a little under 900°C and with almost no melting range. Such an alloy would be excellent for joining components made of alpha brass. Unlike the alloys of silver and copper, the phase diagram of brass shows no lowering of the common melting point below that of each constituent metal. The more zinc added to copper, the lower will be the resulting melting point until the melting temperature of pure zinc is reached. The melting points of pure copper and pure zinc are joined by what for this discussion is essentially a simple curve.

Until zinc was available as a metal and could be alloyed directly with either copper or brass (creating such zinc-rich alloys as pinchbeck, Muntz metal, and Prince Rupert's metal) the practical upper limit of zinc concentration during production of brass was around 30 per cent. Before the advent of high zinc alloys the preferred solder for joining brass was therefore the silver–copper, silver–brass alloy mentioned below for use on silver. Its melting could be adjusted over a wide range, it was malleable and, when highly polished, was almost indistinguishable from the surrounding brass.[2] It was only in the eighteenth century that joining brass with brass became feasible. Klein describes a wide range of solders, again categorized as *schlag* and *schnell*. Among these is

the so-called trumpet-maker solder, which is found in the 9th section of the *Cabinet of Curiosities of Gold and Silver*, page 487, which is made from even parts of brass and zinc. It is described thus: 'Take half spelter [zinc] and half brass, pour them into each other, crush, and mix with Venetian glass and some borax.'[3] (p. 74)

The 'parts' which Klein quotes from the earlier source are presumably by weight as he himself uses the standard measure of Loth (one 256th part of a pound) for which he gives exactly equivalent parts. Assuming the brass contained 25 per cent

---

[2] It would be interesting to analyse the solders of a range of 17th- and 18th- cent. trumpets to see exactly when copper-zinc alloys took over from silver solders.

[3] *Die so genannte Trompetermacherlöthung welche im 9ten Theil der curiösen Schatzkammer von Gold- und Silberarbeiten pag.487 zu finden, rechnen, welche aus gleichen Theilen Messing, und Zink gemacht wird. Es heisst daselbst: 'Nimm halb Spiauter und halb Messing, lass es mit einander fliessen, granulire, stosse und vermische es mit Venedischen Glass und etwas Borras.'*

zinc,[4] this would give a brazing material with 62.5 per cent zinc and 37.5 per cent copper which has a narrow melting range and a melting point of 830°C, over 100°C lower than the best alpha brass. This matches very closely the 60–40 brazing spelter currently available. Although this is an easy-flowing alloy with a conveniently low melting point, it is not very malleable, or 'hammerable'. Although this is an obvious disadvantage in making a trumpet bell, it may be that stresses built up in the solder during hammering are relieved during the frequent annealing which is necessary.

The addition of Venetian glass to the flux indicates a necessary expedient when using metallic zinc. As well as acting as a flux in its own right, the glass fuses on heating into a viscous immobile mass, preventing excessive evaporation of the zinc until it has diffused into the join. It is always advisable when using solders containing zinc to avoid reheating the work as the zinc concentration in the alloy will fall and the surface will become pitted.

Klein describes a range of seventeen sample brass–zinc and copper–zinc solders for brass, the hardest of which contains sixteen parts brass and only one part zinc, giving a zinc concentration scarcely above that of the material to be joined (p. 71). The softest contains but one part of copper to fifteen parts of zinc and could hardly fall into the category of *Schlaglothe* at all as the high-zinc brasses are notoriously brittle (pp. 79–80). The *Trompetermacherlöthung* falls a little over mid-way between these. Five alloys for soft soldering are mentioned (pp. 80–2), and Klein also recommends the addition of tin to copper–zinc and brass–zinc alloys (p. 83).

Klein discusses the use of alloys of both brass with zinc and copper with zinc. It is difficult to understand the distinction he draws between the two, unless his knowledge of the true nature of brass is faulty, as suggested in Chapter 3. Whatever the case, the use of finely powdered brass would be most convenient in any brass workshop because it would be a waste product in plentiful supply. Indeed, bench sweepings are obliquely referred to as a basis for solder in an early nineteenth-century text: 'The powder is ground with a stone wetted in water and dipped in the dust which collects on the [brass worker's] workbench'[5] (Krünitz, 407).

The wide range of melting temperatures and choice of alloys in pre-Industrial Revolution solders (witness the vast number and choice itemized by Klein) developed for very good reasons. In many metalworking applications there is a need for

---

[4] Because zinc is very prone to evaporation when its alloys are heated, it is difficult to estimate the final concentration in a soldering application. Even though Biringuccio, Klein, and others specify brass which we can assume to contain as much as 30% zinc, some loss during heating is inevitable. The figure of 25% is an approximation.

[5] *vornehmlich wenn es mit einem Büschelchen Zeuge (bouchon d'étoffe) gerieben ist, das man mit Wasser nass gemacht, und in Staub getunktet hat, der sich auf dem Werkbrete sammelt.* (This is a passing and somewhat vague reference, but the practice of using bench sweepings for solder was apparently very common for obvious economical reasons.)

TABLE 3 *Historical solders for brass*

Author	Silver	Copper	Zinc	Tin	Melting point (°C)
Trompetenmacherlot	00.0	37.5	62.5	00.0	830
Klein	00.0	33.3	33.3	33.3	~740
Klein	00.0	66.6	33.3	00.0	930
Klein	5.8	53.0	41.2	00.0	870
Muntz Metal	00.0	60.0	40.0	00.0	895
Klein*	57.0	32.0	11.0	00.0	670
Slik Sil 106	55.0	35.0	10.0	00.0	660

Notes: Several of the solders for silver shown in Table 4 were used also for brass and other non-ferrous metals; a silver solder described by Klein (marked with an asterisk) is added to this table for comparison. Note that where zinc is added to the solder unwittingly as a constituent of brass, a figure of 25% zinc/75% copper is used. Where it is added as a metal, it is assumed to be pure. For example, Klein uses the term *Spiauter* which we may assume to be the cognate of spelter, the old term for zinc. (Zinc and copper oxides are sometimes specified, rather than the pure metals, but the terminology is somewhat vague.) Note also that the melting point in this table is the point at which melting *begins*.

serial assembly. The first component may be attached with a high melting point solder, the second is then attached with a somewhat 'faster' alloy to avoid detaching the first, and a third component may even be added at a still lower melting point. The control of the fire to complete successfully all three operations required the skill of a true master. The section describing the assembly of the more elaborately decorated bell garlands (Chapter 6 under 'The Garland') gives an example of such a serial assembly. All the above solders appear in Table 3.

Solders for Silver

The most common solder for silver from antiquity to the present is an alloy of silver and copper, with the addition of other metals to lower its melting point further and to promote easy flowing. The phase diagram for silver–copper alloys (see Fig. 29) shows the two terminal solid solutions at elevated temperatures, the two phase alloy over almost all of the mixing range, and the two semi-solid zones. When the alloy is heated to a temperature between the solidus and liquidus points the constituent metals behave differently from each other. A line drawn at, say, 70 per cent copper will pass through a zone where solid copper contains liquid silver. On the other hand, at 20 per cent copper a line will pass through a similar zone, but in reverse, where solid silver contains liquid copper. In both cases the alloy passes through a semi-solid range upon heating.

In the mixing ratio of some alloys there is a point where they behave like single metals, melting and flowing at a single temperature. Solidus and liquidus occur at one temperature and the liquid and solid phases contain the same proportions of the two metals. This is called the eutectic point. The eutectic point of silver and copper is at 780°C when the alloy contains 72 per cent silver and 28 per cent copper. A line drawn vertically on the copper–silver phase diagram will pass from the solid phase to the liquid phase with no transition. It will be noticed that the eutectic point of this alloy is lower than the melting points of both constituents (961°C for silver and 1083°C for copper). However, depression of the melting point of the alloy below those of its major constituents can also be done by addition of a third metal. For example, the addition of zinc to a copper–silver alloy (or perhaps the addition of brass to silver, which the early craftsmen would have understood better) causes a further lowering of the melting point, or melting range. A corresponding proportion of tin added to copper–silver will depress the melting point further.

The silver solders developed in prehistory continued in use virtually unchanged until comparatively recently; once formulated and tried there was scarcely any way of improving them. For this reason recipes from sources centuries, and sometimes millenia, apart contain similar information. The *Mappae Clavicula*, the recipes of which apparently date from antiquity, describes a silver solder composed of '2 pennyweight and an obol of the purest copper, and 1 pennyweight of silver'. Another recipe calls for '2 parts of silver and a third part of copper' to which is added a little tin (p. 67). These two recipes provide for both hard and relatively soft solders for silver. Theophilus, writing perhaps a millenium later, recommends 'two parts of silver and a third of red copper' (p. 107). This is the same solder which Benvenuto Cellini (1568) calls *terzo* because of its two-plus-one mixing proportions (p. 11). This, quite obviously, gives an alloy of 66.6 per cent silver and 33.3 per cent copper, very close to the eutectic point. Biringuccio says that 'The solder is made from fine silver with a half brass and a quarter burned copper, broken into small pieces' (p. 365). Zinc is unwittingly included, producing a ternary alloy with better wetting characteristics. If it is assumed again that the brass contained 25 per cent zinc, this results very approximately in an alloy of 57 per cent silver, 35.5 per cent copper, and 7.5 per cent zinc. Its melting range would be around 785°C and thus considerably lower than that of silver, although about the same as the eutectic for silver and copper alone.

In the eighteenth century Klein describes a very wide range of solders for silver, depending upon the application and the required durability. An equivalent solder to the one described by Biringuccio contains four parts of fine silver (i.e. silver with no additional copper) to three parts of brass (p. 38). Assuming again that the brass contained 25 per cent zinc, this would give an alloy of 57 per cent silver, 32 per cent copper and 11 per cent zinc. He also describes, among many others, a soft solder

TABLE 4 *Historical solders for silver*

Author	Silver	Copper	Zinc	Melting point (°C)
Mappae Clavicula	66.6	33.3	0.0	800
Theophilus	66.6	33.3	0.0	800
Cellini	66.6	33.3	0.0	800
Biringuccio	57.0	35.5	0.0	785
Klein	57.0	32.0	11.0	760
Klein	6.0	53.0	41.0	875

Notes: Note that where zinc is added to the solder unwittingly as a constituent of brass, a figure of 25% zinc/75% copper is used. Where it is added as a metal, it is assumed to be pure. For example, Klein uses the term *Spiauter* which we may assume to be the cognate of spelter, the old term for zinc. (Zinc and copper oxides are sometimes specified, rather than the pure metals, but the terminology is somewhat vague.) Note also that the melting point in this table is the point at which melting *begins*.

containing one part fine silver, 12 parts brass and 4 parts zinc (p. 41). This produces a solder with approximately 6 per cent silver, 53 per cent copper, and 41 per cent zinc. All the above solders appear in Table 4.

Ideal Properties of a Solder

Ideally a solder should have the following characteristics.

- Melting point suitable to the application. The melting point is usually chosen to be as high as possible under the circumstances—close to the melting point of the metal for hard solders, and close to the melting point of other components for soft solders.
- Suitable flow range for the application. An alloy close to eutectic will flow very readily and then freeze rapidly, while one with a wider range will be more sluggish. The closeness of the join dictates the melting range required.
- Good wetting properties. A matching surface energy will ensure good wetting, which will, in turn, enhance penetration of the alloy into the substrate.
- Adequate strength. The strength must be matched to the application. Hard solder is required for joints which will be worked further, or which take considerable loads. Soft solder may be all that is required for decorative elements.
- Reasonable malleability. The malleability of an alloy can rarely be matched exactly to that of the components to be joined, but its capacity to deform must be within the same range to avoid cracking or distortion.

The practical application of these materials to the components of trumpets is dealt with in Chapter 6.

Fluxes

All common metals except gold form a film of oxide, especially when heated. By combining with the atoms at the surface the oxide provides the metal with a satisfactorily low energy state, thus preventing alloying with other metals. In order to prevent oxidation on heating a flux is used on solder joints. The flux has two functions: first, it acts as a scavenger for surface oxides, dissolving them away and cleaning the metal surface; secondly, it acts as a protective film over the metal until the liquid solder comes in contact. The flux must have enough affinity to the surface to remain in place during heating, yet be sufficiently weak that when the molten solder arrives it will be uniformly displaced.

A number of mineral, vegetable and animal materials have been used as soldering fluxes. Among these are borax, lees of wine (tartar), salt, sal ammoniac, tree resins and tallow. Their specific use depends upon the temperature range over which they are effective. Resins and tallow are suitable only for soft soldering as they soon burn and become ineffective. Sal ammoniac (NH_4Cl) vapourizes at 340°C and is therefore useful for the low to middle range. Higher-temperature fluxes include lees of wine and borax.

Lees of wine (or *Weinstein*) is a crude sodium potassium tartrate ($NaKC_4O_6 \cdot \frac{1}{4} H_2O$), a reaction product of the tartaric acid in grapes. It is scraped out of wine vats, dried, and ground into a fine powder. It is sometimes known in English as argol. Its use as a soldering flux is mentioned by Theophilus (p. 107), Birunguccio (p. 365), and Klein (p. 92), among others.

The most common flux for hard soldering from the Renaissance until the present was sodium tetraborate ($Na_2B_4O_7 \cdot 10H_2O$), or borax, a name derived from the Arabic *bauraq* meaning white. It is a naturally occurring mineral which was apparently first imported into Europe from the saline lakes of Kashmir and Tibet by Marco Polo in the thirteenth century. Theophilus appears to mention borax, or something like it, but there is some confusion as he refers to it as a resin (p. 105). Occasionally borax was pre-treated by first heating it until it fused and then grinding the mass in a mortar and pestle. This drove off the water of crystallization associated with the molecule ($10H_2O$) and prevented excess bubbling on heating. As pointed out earlier, it was common practice to grind the flux with the solder components and apply them as one to the work. Soldering techniques are described in some detail in Chapter 6.

5

The Workshop

I see no more Reason, why the Sordidness of some Workmen, should be the
cause of contempt upon Manual Operations, than that the excellent Invention
of a Mill should be dispis'd, because a blind Horse draws in it.

Joseph Moxon

Introduction

The two direct depictions of the trumpet-maker's workshop are by Weigel of 1698
(Fig. 30) and Diderot and d'Alembert of *c.* 1765[1] (Fig. 31). Of the two, Weigel is the
more appropriate in date and location and would be of the most use were it not for
the untrustworthy rendering of some details. It is easy to confuse realistic appearance in an illustration with accurate depiction. (This has led to the reconstruction
of some pretty fantastic musical instruments.) Although the Renaissance ideal of
rendering from experience supplanted the medieval concept of working from an *ex-
emplum* (Panofsky, 277), this does not mean that the information in graphic studies
became suddenly more reliable. For example, while the realism in perspective, atmosphere, and space of fifteenth-century Flemish painting is plain to see, a few examples show that this does not extend to details. The alignment of the tubing of one
of Memlinc's famous 'slide trumpets' is far from accurate,[2] the angel organist in Van
Eyck's altarpiece is playing an instrument improperly scaled, and so on. Also, art-
historical theories applied to the stylistic trends of great works of art cannot necessarily be transferred to minor book illustrations. If one examines the trumpet and
the horn hanging on the wall in Weigel's illustration a lack of accuracy in almost
every respect is evident. Both instruments are so poorly rendered that they give one
a key to the rest of the picture; if these fairly common objects, the chief subject of
the text, are so far from true, what of the other details in the illustration? Clearly,

[1] This is the approximate date of publication of the volume containing the description of the *Chaudronnier's*
workshop.

[2] A ruler placed along the tubes as they pass under the angel's hand will show that none align properly with each
other. This has not deterred the making of eccentric reproductions which try to emulate this feature.

F IG. 30. The master trumpet-maker's workshop illustrated by Christoph Weigel in *Abbil-dung der gemein nützlichen Hauptstände* (Regensberg, 1698). Note that both the partially finished bell resting diagonally on the bench and the mandrels on the wall rack are well depicted, while the instruments hanging on the wall are very poorly rendered

for safety in interpretation it is necessary to provide corroboration for all other features.

Diderot's illustration comes late in the period of this study, and depicts actions in France not Germany. More to the point, all the instruments illustrated in process of construction (in the top Fig.) are horns, which, in view of the complete absence of extant French trumpets, probably represents the true situation. However, most hand tools have not changed significantly since Classical times, so when making comparisons with Weigel's illustration, a rendering a mere century and six hundred kilometres distant can be assumed to contain essentially the same information.

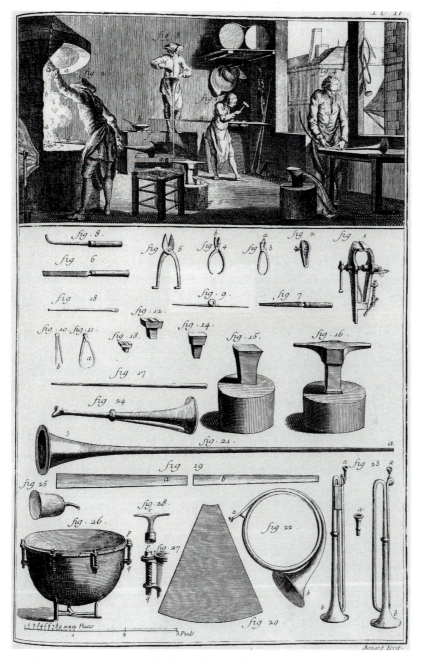

FIG. 31. The brass instrument maker's workshop from the section on the *Chaudronnier* of Diderot and d'Alembert's *Encyclopédie*, Paris, *c.*1765. The tools are accurately depicted but the workshop concentrates on horns, not trumpets

In fact, the French source is more reliable in the rendering of details because by the middle of the eighteenth century the heightened belief in the inherent order and rationale of the universe at large was expressing itself in meticulous attention to detail, physical as well as philosophical. Even so, there are still cautions: why is the craftsman at the forge putting the narrow end of a bell in the fire and pulling vigorously at the bellows lanyard? Because this depicts the actual process of soldering, or because the worker strikes a classically expressive pose?

The Workspace

An interesting observation on the layout of the workshop and the division of labour arises from the two illustrations of brass instrument-makers at work. Diderot and d'Alembert illustrate a shop floor where a certain degree of mass production is taking place. There are four workers, each engaged in a particular operation. While the four figures may serve simply to illustrate four separate phases of production, it is far more likely that a production line is in operation. On the other hand, it is certain that the picture of comparative leisure which Christoph Weigel shows is that of a master in his personal workshop, engaged on a special commission. The most significant feature of this depiction is the lack of a forge. Weigel's illustrator did not forget to include it; he simply did not see one in the master's workshop. This strongly suggests that the master would have the rough preparatory work done for him on the shop floor. He would then finish, assemble, and decorate.[3] If this is true, it is indeed fortuitous that the only two half-way reliable illustrations of the trumpet-maker's domain show both areas—the frenetic activity of the shop floor and the more sedate pace of the master trumpet-maker's own shop. As pointed out in Chapter 2, the demarcation is, of course, visible in the variable quality of the finished products. This discussion will be taken up later in the chapter when working conditions are examined.

Workshop Layout

It is pointless to be too analytical on the layout of the workshop because so much would depend upon available space, number of personnel, and so on, but a few generalizations will help set the scene. In the absence of artificial light the workday would coincide with daylight hours. Large, high windows facing south would there-

---

[3] The fact that the master is wielding a hammer does not indicate that he regularly made bells; the artist has chosen to render the trumpet-maker's most characteristic pose for his illustration.

fore be a necessity.[4] The lathes, and benches for fine work like engraving and polishing, would be as close as possible to the light, and the layout table for marking and cutting sheet brass would also be along this side. (All the fine craftsmen illustrated by Jost Amman sit at open windows while passers-by look in.) Adjacent to these benches, and within easy reach, there would be racks for the tools, patterns, and templates used in each task. Behind these benches, in the centre of the room, would be work sites for forming and finishing tubing and bells, bending bows, and soldering components. On the opposite wall from the windows would be the forge surrounded by quenching troughs, anvils and stakes, and racks for the forge tools. It is essential to have the forge in a darker area, the better to judge the colours of the metal when heating. In the corner of the workshop would be a separate enclosure, amply supplied with light and fresh air, where the master had his workshop. Close to this would be the office and 'shop front' of the establishment. Further than this it is not wise to speculate.

Tool Steel

Almost all the trumpet-maker's tools had to be made of a hard, durable material; burins for engraving needed to hold a very fine, hard edge, files and sawblades required reliable cutting edges, and hammers, punches, and anvils took a fearful beating. Although iron served as the basic material for tool-making, its transformation into steel by the addition of carbon was a necessary stage in the production of durable tools. There were two basic processes: an earlier process called cementation, and the newer development of mixing high and low carbon fractions. The products were also called, respectively, blister steel and crucible steel.

The conversion of iron to steel by cementation was initially an accidental process. During smelting of iron ore with charcoal, and the subsequent hammering of the iron-carbon mixture called 'bloom', it was inevitable that a certain proportion of carbon would be incorporated into the iron. The steel so formed contained between 0.5 and 1.5 per cent carbon and if quenched in water from red heat would be much harder than the iron from which it came. This was sometimes called 'pack hardening'. Also, the presence of phosphorus in some iron ores caused the iron to harden on working.

As well as naturally produced 'steel', craftsmen had been 'case hardening' iron tools since at least antique times; this was a kind of cementation where the iron tool

---

[4] The north light so favoured by painters is weaker but gives a better colour balance and is more uniform with changes in weather. Craftsmen preferred bright southern illumination.

was coated with a flux with the addition of charcoal, charred horn shavings, or even leather scraps. It was then encased in clay and heated in a furnace, which caused the carbon from the organic material to diffuse into the iron. This produced a tool with a soft iron core and a very thin hardened surface. The process of cementation was deliberately applied in Renaissance Germany: iron was embedded in charcoal in a closed container and heated for as long as forty-eight hours to cause diffusion into the mass. If carried to completion this produced a true steel, not simply a case hardening. Although developed in the German-speaking regions, iron from Sweden and Spain was apparently favoured for this process due to its low phosphorus content. (The presence of phosphorus in iron retards the diffusion of carbon.) Swedish steel for tools was in demand over the whole of Europe for several centuries after its appearance.

Following the development of more efficient blast-furnaces in Germany from the sixteenth century onwards, iron could be made to reach its melting point, around 1,200°C, and as much as 4 per cent carbon would then be absorbed, forming the brittle substance known as pig-iron. This could then be reheated and the excess carbon oxidized away by an air blast, producing a soft, malleable iron. In order to produce a tool steel with just the right amount of carbon, Continental ironsmiths developed a technique of mixing a certain proportion of pig-iron (with a high carbon content) with refined low-carbon iron. The steel thus produced became an extremely marketable international commodity for a few centuries until the technique became more widely adopted.

The steel which the tool-makers of Nuremberg used for their raw material might have been made by any of the above techniques. Where hardness of the surface only was necessary (e.g. for files) the case hardening of iron described above would be sufficient. Tougher tools, like punches and burins, would be made of steel stock supplied by the foundries and produced either by cementation or mixing. In making and sharpening a steel tool the stock would first be annealed by heating and slow cooling to make it workable. Once sawn, ground, or filed to shape it underwent a two-stage hardening and tempering process. Heating to dull red heat and then quenching in water made it 'glass hard', then after polishing (to judge the correct colour) it was heated gently to a pale yellow or brown and quickly quenched. (Yellow is hardest, but brittle, while blue is tough but not as able to hold a sharp edge.) Urine or salt solutions were sometimes favoured over water for quenching, apparently because the steel cools marginally slower in a solution than it does in pure water.[5] Similarly, oil and sometimes sealing wax were used to retard cooling. After tempering, the tool would be tough, but not brittle. Nevertheless, the hardest steel

---

[5] When the author worked in Clerkenwell, London, in the 1960s there was an old established blacksmith who always urinated into his quenching trough. As well as the convenience this gave in his rather primitive establishment, he stated that his father and grandfather had done this and it 'made the iron harder'.

available to the seventeenth- and eighteenth-century craftsman could not rival the special alloys which exist today. Neither were blades, drills, and other components ever regarded as disposable, as they often are today. Great skill in sharpening and maintaining tools was a prerequisite of the competent trumpet-maker. In fact, the larger workshops may have employed an ironsmith who had the responsibility of making mandrels and specialized tools not available on the open market, and also of sharpening and maintaining tools.

The Tools

The trumpet-makers shared tools, techniques, and suppliers with many other metalworking crafts and trades in Nuremberg. A great many of the common tools were manufactured and offered for sale by specialists. Illustrations of the huge range of tools available can be found in the *Ständebuch* of Jost Amman and Hans Sachs, who actually illustrate the tool-maker's shop (p. 70) although with scant details. Some excellent material can be found in Hartmann Schopper's *De Omnibus Illiberalis* of the mid-sixteenth century, while Joseph Moxon describes tools and techniques in great detail in *Mechanick Exercises* of 1703.

In addition to off-the-shelf tools, each craft had its own special tools and templates which were the property of the craftsmen and were jealously guarded. Regarding tools specifically for trumpet-making, the illustrations published in Augsburg in 1740 by Martin Engelbrecht of the *Trompeten, Posaunen und Waldhornmacher* and the *Trompetenmacherin* (Figs. 32 and 33) show the apparatus at a fairly late stage in its development. However, most of the tools shown had been in use for hundreds of years and can be regarded as typical. Among these tools and equipment are several items not shown by either Diderot or Weigel. Because the figures are static, no clue is given in these illustrations to the techniques.

One of the tasks of a journeyman would be making a set of mandrels and templates under the master's close scrutiny. Such rods as were necessary for the yards might last a lifetime, but bell mandrels and sheet metal templates might need replacement as bell profiles changed according to the dictates of musical style and performance.

Following is an inventory of the tools which were required for making trumpets in the seventeenth- and eighteenth-century workshops of Nuremberg. Most of these are illustrated by either Weigel, Diderot, or Englebrecht, although there are occasional omissions. Where necessary, corroboration is provided from the other contemporary sources mentioned above, or illustrations are provided from the author's own set of tools. The specific use of these tools in trumpet-making will be discussed in Chapter 6.

FIG. 32. Engraving entitled *Trompeten, Posaunen und Waldhornmacher* by Martin Engelbrecht, published in Augsburg in 1740. The inventory of tools here is very complete. (Courtesy of Ernst W. Buser, Binningen, and Trompetenmuseum, Bad Säckingen)

FIG. 33. Engraving entitled *Trompetenmacherin* by Martin Engelbrecht, published in Augsburg in 1740. This figure is highly allegorical as the very idea of a lady working in a metal shop borders on the ludicrous. Note the winch on the lady's head and the softly curled sheet of brass which serves as a 'hair piece'. (Courtesy of Ernst W. Buser, Binningen, and Trompetenmuseum, Bad Säckingen)

Templates

Calibrated measuring tools were scarce in the Renaissance workshop, but through
the seventeenth and eighteenth centuries the demands of astronomical and survey-
ing instrument-makers accelerated development of precision measuring devices.[6]
Nevertheless, in the brass musical-instrument workshop all sizing of parts was done
by direct comparison with standards. For example, lengths of components would
be gauged against marks on the workbench, diameters would be established by the
size of mandrels used in forming, and each piece of brass sheet would be marked
out from a template of that exact size. Templates were probably made from sheet
iron for durability and cheapness. The craftsman would lay the template on the
brass sheet and mark around it with a sharp steel scriber. Engelbrecht's two figures
are both carrying bell templates at their belts (Nos. 15 and 8 in his illustrations).

Mandrels

All sheet metal parts of a trumpet were made up on mandrels and the pieces stayed
on those mandrels during almost all operations. The straight tubes were originally
formed around straight iron rods, some of which can be seen resting diagonally
below the shelf in the background of Weigel's illustration. Later, a corrugated plate
was used in conjuction with the rods, as carried at the waist of Engelbrecht's male
figure. Bells were finish-formed by burnishing (not hammering) on shaped mandrels, three of which can be seen on the rack in the rear.[7] The long spindles projecting from the wide ends are an indication that the bell, mounted on its mandrel,
might be turned on the lathe as a final step in polishing (see 'The Wheel Lathe',
below). Engelbrecht's mandrels also have generous spindles. Each style of trumpet
(and trombone) would require its own mandrel. Mandrels needed a relatively hard
surface but as no hammering was ever done on them they did not need to be as
durable as the anvils, for example. Steel was very expensive—two to three times the
cost of iron—so good quality wrought iron was used and then case hardened to provide a hard working surface. Mandrels were forged and filed to rough shape and
then turned on the lathe before hardening. The accuracy of these turnings is not
known, but Charles Plumier mentioned in his book of 1701 that he knew of only
two other turners who could work accurately in iron (Bedini and Price, 183).

---

[6] Herbert Heyde provides information on the system of measurement used by the craftsmen of Nuremberg in
Musikinstrumentenbau, 74 (see *Bibliography*).
[7] Several modern trumpet-makers have hammered bells on mandrels and there is even a television programme
where this is seen in progress. This is entirely wrong; although this can be done on mandrels of modern steel, it
would be detrimental to those of case-hardened iron.

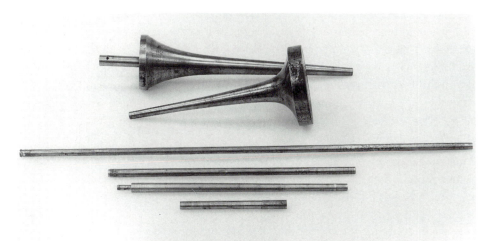

FIG. 34. A set of mandrels for making two styles of trumpet—a shallow flared bell of the early 17th-cent., and a sharply flared bell of *c.*1700. Note that both bell mandrels are only half the length of the finished bell. This was done for economy in machining; in use, the extensions (shown below the long mandrel) which fit into the bellpipe are screwed into place. Also shown are mandrels for the yards and garnishes

In addition to mandrels for forming sheet metal, all the parts for turning would have to be attached to mandrels which fitted between the centres of the lathe. For example, the tubular garnishes fit snugly over a parallel steel mandrel which supports them during machining, and especially prevents collapse when designs are embossed on them. The concentric engraving on the bell garland also requires the use of a conical mandrel which can be run on the lathe, although this can be made of hard wood (Fig. 34).

The Forge

The most conspicuous, although entirely explicable, absence from Weigel's illustration is the forge; one is shown in the workshop of the *faiseur d'instruments*, although tucked away to the side. The forge consists of a flat bed for coals with a central depression called a tuyère through which air is blasted from the bellows. The bellows are hand pumped by the smith, or by a labourer during complex processes. In earlier times the smoke from the forge might simply find its way out of an aperture in the crest of the roof, although in the later workshops there would be a hood above the coals leading to a chimney to extract smoke and fumes from the workplace. Some forges were even built into walls like elevated fireplaces, complete

with stone or brick chimneys. Since brass and solders melt at a fairly low temperature it would be essential to locate the forge in a semi-dark place to observe colour
changes. A rack was situated near the forge for holding tongs, shovels, pokers, and
hammers. Close by was a quenching trough filled with water. There would also be
a trough filled with pickling solution for cleaning brass and removing borax after
soldering.

Soldering Equipment

Most soldering of components was done 'in the fire'—pieces were coated with the
solder-flux mixture, held together with wires, and heated in the coals. In order to
ensure even distribution of heat, red-hot coals had to be piled over the object to be
soldered. A perforated iron bowl or trough (depending upon the shape of the work)
was first placed over the object and hot coals could then be piled on to this without
fear of touching the work. During heating the workman could peer through one of
the perforations to check on progress (Maryon, 33–4). Fine work, however, was
done at a soldering bench using a hot coal held in a pair of tongs, over which was
directed a blowpipe. Klein shows a very elegant soldering bench with foot-operated
bellows (Fig. 35). Engelbrecht's two figures both carry a *Känlein*, or little can, at
their belts. These were filled with a mixture of flux and finely granulated solder, a
practice still followed by some jewellers today.

Anvils and Stakes

The metalworker in the *Abbildung* is working on a form of anvil which fits into a
socket cut in a firm, solid block, usually a cross-section of a whole tree trunk. Martin Engelbrecht shows this even more clearly. In both cases it is not a true anvil as
it is removable from its socket and has a shape specifically tailored for its application. It is better referred to as a stake. In Weigel's picture three spare stakes rest on
the floor at the worker's feet. The artist has failed to differentiate between the sizes
of stakes as smaller ones with differently shaped heads are necessary for some operations.[8] See, for example, the two very differently shaped heads in the *Encyclopédie*
illustration which also shows three small purpose-built stakes. The low, squat
'anvil' on the right is called a beaker iron. The expense of steel made it necessary to
forge-weld a steel working surface on to a wrought iron anvil body. Although anvils
and stakes had hard steel surfaces, they might still become deformed with long use.
It would, therefore, make good sense to reserve one large stake in a highly polished
condition for the final light hammer work on the bell—the planishing which
smoothed out dents left by the heavier forming.

[8] Weigel does differentiate in the text; he refers to both the *Ambos* and the *Becher-Eisen.*

FIG. 35. A bench for fine soldering from J. G. F. Klein's *Beschreibung der Metall-Lothe und Löthungen*, (Berlin 1760). The bench is complete with a foot-operated bellows for pumping the blowpipe

Hammers and Mallets

Several sizes and weights of hammers were necessary, from the heavy pegging hammer, which was used for the initial flaring of the bell, to smaller ones for planishing, wrinkle removal on the insides of the bows, forming balls, and turning over garland edges. Hammers always had hardened steel faces forge-welded on to wrought-iron bodies. The handles were of wood to give springiness and absorb mechanical shock. The hammer Weigel's trumpet-maker is using is the typical pegging hammer for the initial forming of the bell. It has a relatively short handle for accuracy of attack and a long head to give sufficient mass. The shape of the head has a bearing on the direction in which metal will flow when struck. These hammers usually have a rectangular head so that metal can be pushed in a specific direction. This is dealt with in detail in Chapter 6.

Mallets, on the other hand, are made of wood or densely packed rawhide and are used where no damage to the metal can be countenanced. In the background of Diderot's illustration the worker is using a small wood mallet to wrap sheet metal

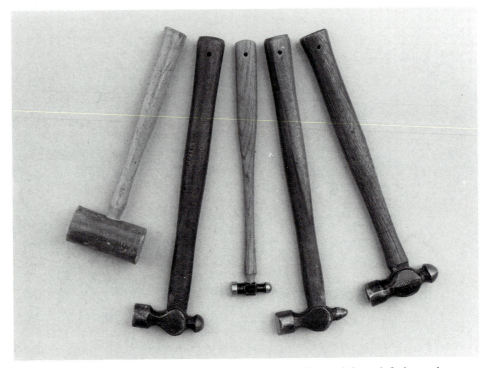

Fig. 36. A set of hammers from the author's workshop. From right to left: heavy hammer with rounded edges for initial forming of bells; hammer with rounded head for reducing wrinkles on the inside of bows; general purpose ball pein hammer; lightweight hammer with curved, highly polished head for turning bell rims and other light finishing work; and rawhide mallet for light forming

around a mandrel. (Note that the mandrel is conveniently attached to the wall.) The mallet on Weigel's workbench is over-large for most jobs, but those sported by Engelbrecht's lady and gentleman are much better proportioned. A range of useful hammers is shown in Fig. 36.

Punches

Garnishes, rim bezels, and garlands all carry punched designs. Punches were made from tool steel carved and filed to the desired shape and then hardened and tempered by heating and quenching. Embossed designs on the garnishes were punched with the component in place on a mandrel. When embossing the very popular scallopshells on the garland, it would be laid on a block of lead and the punch driven with the hammer from the reverse side. Punched designs are common on a variety of artefacts so it is likely that a wide selection of punches could be bought from suppliers. Punched patterns characteristic of certain makers may, however, have been their exclusive property. By the end of the eighteenth century some makers used commercial letter punches for the name and date on the bell garland.

Crucible and Ladle for Lead

In order to bend thin-walled tubing it is first filled with lead to prevent its collapse. In the rear of Diderot's illustration a worker is filling a horn from the bell end prior to bending. Lead is transferred from the crucible at his feet to the work by a metal ladle. Pitch could also be used, instead of lead, as the curves in the tubing of horns are quite shallow. In either case a crucible and ladle are necessary. Engelbrecht shows this equipment very well, to his *Trompetenmacher*'s left.

Bending Jigs

There are several ways of bending tubing filled with lead or pitch. One of the *faiseurs d'instruments* is seen simply bending it between his thumbs and fingers, using the bench to press down on. For the gentle curves of the horn this is quite sufficient. For trumpet bows a jig is required. Some modern restorers and makers use a radiused hole in a block of hard wood (Menzel, *MICAT*, facing p. 39). Others use a block curved to the required finished shape of the bow around which to bend the tubing (Fig. 37). Weigel shows a curious device on the left side of the anvil block which could be a bending jig. The curved 'plate' attached to its upper surface approximates the correct curvature, but its exact use is conjectural.

Vices

Two kinds of vice were in use in metalwork shops; the leg vice, which was attached to the bench and had an extension to the floor, and the hand vice, which was used for holding small items. A small hand vice is shown by Engelbrecht on the anvil block, and Diderot shows another. As seen in the illustration from Moxon (see Fig. 38), the bench vice was used on occasions for holding a small lathe for fine work. Mandrels could also be gripped while parts were being worked upon. The jaws, or chaps, of a vice can be seen just in front of the lathe in the illustration in Fig. 30, although this is a very inconvenient position for the vice, and it lacks a turnscrew for tightening. The type illustrated by Diderot is typical of the all-metal model which became increasingly popular in the eighteenth century. If it was ever necessary to grip brass components, the jaws would be padded with hard wood, copper, or lead in order to avoid damage.

F IG. 37. Three simple wooden bending jigs from the author's workshop. To use the jig at the top, the lead-filled tube is inserted in the hole and bent around the curved form. The circular jig at bottom right is use for bending the full circles of crooks. The radiused wood block at the bottom left is the most versatile of these jigs

Pliers and Tongs

Several sizes and shapes of pliers were used, including the common flat nosed and pointed nosed types. They were of good-quality steel, where economically possible, and would be virtually identical to those in use today. Where good steel was too expensive tool-makers often forge-welded steel cutting edges on to wrought iron tools. Weigel shows two pairs of pliers in the rack at the rear, apparently one of each kind. The illustrations in the *Encyclopédie* are much more reliable. Tongs were a cruder form of tool altogether; they were made of wrought iron only and were used at the forge for handling hot metal and crucibles.

Lathes

During the period under discussion the lathe was undergoing a huge transformation in the hands of such inventors as Jacques Besson, engineer to Charles IX of France (Bedini and Price, 181). There were at least three kinds of lathe available to the seventeenth- and eighteenth-century craftsmen, all of which were potentially useful in the various processes of trumpet-making. The basic function of the lathe was to rotate metal parts between two fixed centres, originally called cheeks and now known as the headstock and tailstock, while a tool was used for shaping. Weigel's illustration shows the headstock and the bed of a lathe behind the trumpet-maker's hammer arm and below the bell mandrels on the wall. The three varieties, the bow lathe, the pole lathe, and the wheel lathe, are discussed below.

THE BOW LATHE

This is the smallest type of lathe available and was favoured by jewellers and clock-makers (Fig. 38, bottom). It might well have been used for turning the concentric engravings on the ball and garnishes. Although its motive power, the hand-operated bow and string, is of prehistoric origin, models were still available and used in the early part of this century. The string (in the case of a metal-turning lathe, a leather thong) was wrapped either around the work or a driving pulley and tensioned by the bow. Vigorous back-and-forward motion with the left hand was co-ordinated with hand tooling with the right hand. For concentric engravings, like those on garnishes, the graver or burin sits firmly on a rest close to the work and is brought gently into contact.

THE POLE LATHE

Larger or more resistant work might require the use of a pole lathe (Fig. 38, top). The leather thong is connected between a treadle and a tough, flexible wooden pole. The pole serves the same purpose as the bow, allowing the thong to be tensioned, but the treadle frees both hands for turning and gives leg muscle power to the spindle. Such a lathe would be used for finish turning of mouthpiece castings or perhaps concentric embossing on garnishes and other decorative elements. The illustration in Fig. 38 also shows the cutting tools used with this apparatus. The hooked portion of the tool is placed over the tool rest and against one of the pins shown, and the cutting edge is brought to bear on the metal. This arrangement is necessary for heavier work to prevent chattering and 'snatching' of the tool.

THE WHEEL LATHE

Where the nature of the work demanded, the bow and treadle could be replaced with a belt driven by a large wheel. The wheel could be turned by a labourer but it is quite likely that larger workshops had water-powered machinery. The advantage of this system, apart from the extra power provided, was the continuous and steady rotation of the work; during heavy cutting this is essential. A lathe of this kind might be used for rotating the finished bell on its mandrel to give it an even abrasive polish (Fig. 39). In the eighteenth century (and perhaps earlier) a foot-powered

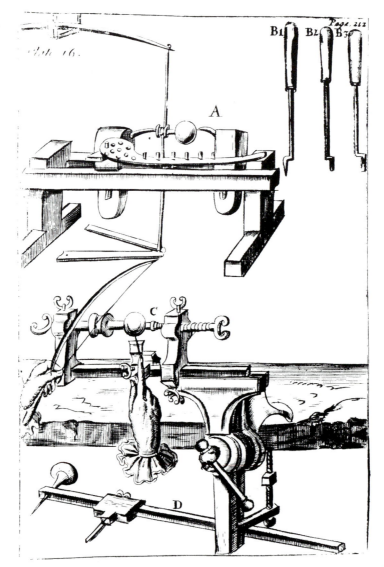

FIG. 38. Illustrations from Joseph Moxon's *Mechanick Exercises or the Doctrine of Handy-Works* (London, 1703), showing two kinds of lathe. The pole lathe at the top is used for medium-sized work while the jeweller's bow lathe, below, is for smaller work. It is generally believed that Moxon did these engravings himself, as their quality is not very high

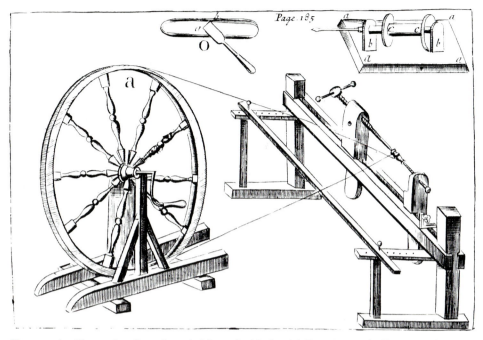

Fig. 39. An illustration from Joseph Moxon's *Mechanick Exercises or the Doctrine of Handy-Works* (London, 1703), showing a large wheel lathe. Such a lathe would be used for rotating the bell when polishing. One of this size might also be powered by water

treadle lathe with a heavy flywheel became available. This was more powerful than the pole lathe but could still be operated by one person.

Drills

Three types of drill were in general use during this period. The bow drill (Fig. 40) was the most common, and it worked in the same way as the bow lathe. The strap drill was a variation on this. These two were used for relatively light work. The drill bits, unlike those of today, had no helical grooves but were simply spade-shaped with a central point. The cutting bit fitted into a square socket in the spindle and the craftsman would have several bits of various sizes. Heavy work was done with the brace, the ancient and fundamentally simple device still familiar today. Almost all work on brass can be done with the former two lightweight drills—the pressure of the brace is too great for fine bits. Applications include the piercing of the bell garland for the stay wire, and decorative features of the garland and garnishes. (The maker of the Haas instrument in Fig. 10 (Chapter 2) could have made his work

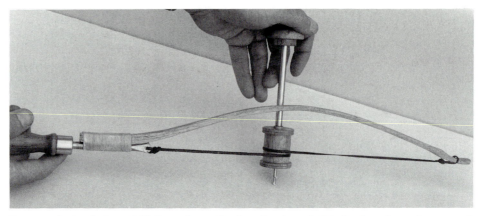

FIG. 40. A simple bow drill from the author's collection. A thin leather thong is wrapped around a pulley which is connected to the drill bit. Backwards and forwards motion of the bow provides the rotation. Drill bits are interchangable. Only a confirmed Luddite would use such a drill in the late 20th cent.

neater by drilling small holes between the embossed scallopshells of the garland before snipping out the excess.)

Tinsnips

Like the pliers, tinsnips achieved their ultimate shape early in the history of technology. Weigel shows three pairs in the same rack as the pliers, Diderot shows only one size, and Englebrecht shows both huge and small pairs. The large straight pair of snips was used for cutting out the sheet brass parts, and a smaller, finer pair, also straight, was used for notching seams, cutting darts in garlands and garnishes, and other detail work. A curved pair would be useful for shaping the sheet metal used for the garland. Like the pliers, only the cutting edges might be of steel. A useful variation on the tinsnips, which none of the above illustrators show, has one handle bent at right angles and fitted into a hole in the workbench. The worker leans his weight on the upper handle while guiding the metal with both hands. Alternatively, one handle of the ordinary tinsnips can be gripped in a vice and used in the same way.

Files

The exceedingly coarse file on the bench shown in the *Abbildung* has been over-drawn for graphic effect. The *Trompetenmacherin*'s files have also been exaggerated for clarity. Generally speaking, fine cut files in a variety of cross-sections—flat, triangular, round, etc.—are the most servicable. File teeth were raised with a chisel in a piece of wrought iron which was then case hardened. The pierced work seen on some of the more decorative bell garlands requires extremely thin and fine files which must have been treasured possessions.

Saws

Only a few trumpet-making operations require the use of a saw; most sheet metal parts are cut out with snips as mentioned above. A lightweight metal saw is useful for cutting bezel wire to length and for trimming excess metal from castings. Tubes were also trimmed to length by sawing while mounted on a steel or iron cut-off rod. The pierced work on the more elaborate bell garlands was done with a frame saw having a thin, flexible blade. Hacksaws with flexible blades are seen in eighteenth century illustrations.

Engraving Tools

Although the finer engraving was probably contracted out, the trumpet workshop would have sets of the simpler tools for the job. Engraving was done with a range of burins (or gravers), tools with diamond-shaped tips which remove metal in a V-shaped groove. The work is finished with a scraper and burnisher. All these tools require very hard steel which is tough and can hold an excellent edge (see Fig. 63).

Drawplates or Swages

Weigel and Diderot both fail to illustrate the steel plate through which tubing was drawn to make it smooth and parallel. This is quite possibly an eighteenth-century adaptation of a much earlier technique, so Weigel may be excused. Engelbrecht shows drawplates very clearly, even to the extent of differentiating hole sizes. The mandrel upon which the tubing had been formed would remain in place during drawing. In spite of the fact that mechanical methods were not generally used in the production of trumpet parts, there is evidence that the yards, at least, were pulled through the swage with a winch device in late eighteenth century workshops. The regularly recurring patterns seen in Fig. 81 were probably formed as a steel die was pulled mechanically over the rough-finished tubing, smoothing it on to the man-drel.[9] They certainly appear too even to be the result of either hand pulling or chat-

---

[9] In an earlier publication (*Preliminary Studies*, 22-3) I had erroneously assumed these marks always to have been caused by burnishing. Although burnishing, which was the standard hand technique, does leave ripples, they are never as uniform as these. During the Industrial Revolution other techniques became applied, including forcing blocks of lead over tapered components to smooth them out, and the use of hydraulic presses for the same purpose, but these need not concern us here.

tering due to scraping. In support of this, the *Trompetenmacherin* has a leather belt with rings at the ends hanging from her waist and a winch on her head (of all places).

Finishing Equipment

All components of the instrument were burnished before final polishing. The burnisher is a heavy rod of hardened steel, highly polished, which is rubbed vigorously over the components mounted on their respective mandrels. Wooden handles attached to the ends of the rod make it comfortable to use. On the yards and bows burnishing serves to give a smooth, even gloss to the metal, while on the bell the effect is to press the brass into firm contact with the mandrel, thus giving both a smooth finish and an accurate and reproducible shape.

The black scale and flux residue on freshly heat-treated brass was probably removed with a scraper if dipping proved ineffective. The scraper is a flat steel blade, sometimes mounted in a wood handle, which removes a thin peeling of the surface. Brass sheet was prepared with a larger version of the same tool by the *Messingschaber* (see Chapter 3).

Polishing can be done quite effectively by scraping followed by burnishing. However, for the more decorative and luxurious specimens further polishing was done with such finely divided abrasive materials as pumice, brick dust, rottenstone, diatomaceous earth (e.g. keiselguhr), kaolin (china clay), whiting, and chalk, all of which were probably used from time to time, depending upon supply and price.[10] These would be mixed into a slurry with water and applied with a cloth or a piece of leather. Sometimes the components were rotated.

The above is a complete inventory of the tools most likely to have been used, although needless to say there must have been variations in both region and time period. Fig. 41 shows a modern set of hand tools (excluding hammers and a drill) which prove to be the minimum necessary for efficient trumpet-making.

Foundry Work

Mouthpieces, angel heads, and decorative features of garnishes and balls on some instruments were all brass castings. These were never made in the trumpet-maker's workshop, but were purchased from foundries with the equipment to produce them

---

[10] Brasso, for example, contains silicon dioxide (a highly abrasive common mineral) and kaolin, which is a milder abrasive derived from the weathering of granite.

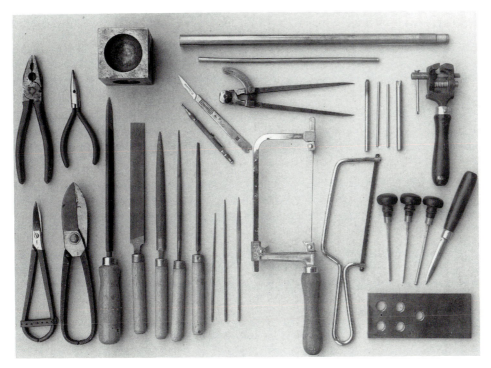

FIG. 41. The minimum hand-tool set (excluding hammers and a drill) required for making historical replicas. At left, two sizes of pliers and two sizes of tinsnips; top left, a dapping block for forming balls; left centre, a triangular scraper and several files of differing profiles and sizes; top centre, two burnishing rods, a pair of dividers and a scriber and knife; right centre, a fine frame saw and a small hacksaw; top right, four punches and a hand vice; right three burins and a burnisher; and bottom right, a swage plate. (The burins are shown in detail in Fig. 64.) All tools are from the author's workshop

en masse. As an example, an order of 12 decorated trumpets would require 48 angel heads, 12 mouthpiece blanks (assuming only one per instrument), 12 balls, and as many as 120 garnish pieces. A foundry which could mass produce such 'findings' by the hundreds was an essential support facility. Such a foundry would not exist solely to support one industry; the brass instrument-makers doubtless decided to place angel heads on their bells because the castings were already available as a stock item to any craftsman who needed them. The angel head is a very popular motif on a wide range of brasswares. Other parts specific to the trumpet were cast by special order; the more pieces the trumpet-maker ordered, the cheaper they would be.

Birunguccio (p. 73–4) provides a very vivid description of the casting of brass findings which he observed in Milan. As many as sixty master patterns of objects

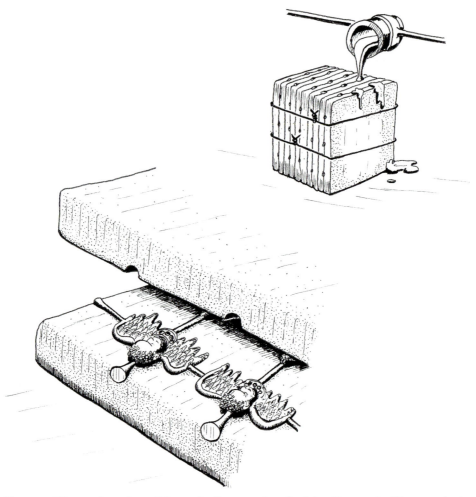

FIG. 42. The casting of small brass findings as described by Vannoccio Birunguccio in *Pirotechnia* of 1540. The master patterns are pressed into clay plates and joined by a network of channels to allow the molten brass to flow between them. Once the master patterns are removed the plates are stacked and wired together and the molten metal is poured in

like belt buckles, chains, thimbles, and window fastenings were pressed into a thin layer of fine clay reinforced with cloth clippings or cane-seed fibres. Once each pattern was pressed into the clay it was connected to the others with vents and gates so that during pouring the molten brass would flow into it without obstruction. Once the patterns were pressed into this lower section, it was baked to harden it and then, with the patterns in place, a top layer of clay mixture was pressed over. Once baked this made the lid of the mould. Removal of the patterns left an air space between the pieces which exactly replicated the detailed shapes of the patterns and the vents. Pairs of these clay plates were stacked up and wired together until a mould for a single pouring might contain a thousand or more individual findings (Fig. 42). 'Pondering on this,' Birunguccio says, 'I thought to myself that this shop alone was sufficient to furnish not only Milan but also the whole of Italy . . .' (p. 74). He further states that he has not seen this process being used elsewhere, but it certainly would have been used in the century following the publication of his description.

Gilding

Components of both brass and silver trumpets were sometimes gold-plated, while brass instruments often had silvered garnishes and other decorative features. It is possible that components were sent out to specialists for this kind of work, especially in the later period when production was at a high level. Although the term 'gilding' is normally used specifically for the application of gold, many other metals, including gold-like bronzes and silver, were also applied. The garnishes and balls of the pair of trumpets by Johann Carl Kodisch in the Germanisches Nationalmuseum (MIR 162 and 163) have been overlaid with silver, for example.

There were two chief ways of plating one metal over another before the development in the nineteenth century of electroplating: amalgam gilding and leaf gilding. Amalgam is by far the most efficient method of applying gold or silver to a base metal because it relies on the solvent property of mercury. The precious metal (either gold or silver) is dissolved in mercury and this is swabbed on to the surface of the metal to be plated. The mercury, carrying the gold or silver with it, penetrates the surface of the base metal, providing an extremely efficient bond. Benvenuto Cellini (*c.*1568) recommends a solution of one part of gold to eight parts of mercury (p. 96), the mercury being warmed in a clean crucible to aid dissolution of the gold. The work to be gilded must be extremely clean and free of oxidation. Brass wire brushes were used to abrade the surface just prior to applying the amalgam, and occasionally abrasives, or acids such as aqua fortis, were used. The gold–mercury solution was applied with a little copper rod set in a wooden handle. Once the coating was complete the piece was set in a slow fire to drive off the mercury as vapour. The gold was then thoroughly bonded to the base metal but, because of vapourization of the mercury, it was quite porous. It then had to be burnished to a high shine with a polished steel burnisher, a hard stone, or, occasionally, a dog's tooth.

Sometimes, instead of mixing the precious metal with mercury, a so-called cold amalgamation was done. In this case the metal to be plated was rubbed with either mercury or a mercury salt and then coated with thin beaten leaves of gold or silver.

It is possible to distinguish between the two methods using microscopical techniques (Raub, p.10). Both gilding processes are illustrated by Diderot in the *Encyclopédie*.

Working Conditions

This chapter would not be complete without mention of the conditions in which brass instruments were made. Amalgam gilding, in particular, raises the question of workshop safety, especially in view of the apparent disregard for the poisonous effects of mercury vapour which the employees in Diderot's illustration show. Cellini, writing in the sixteenth century, had this to say about the gilding trade: 'But none the less I say that great masters ought not to practise this [gilding] themselves, for the quicksilver that has to be used is a deadly poison, and so wears out the men that practise in it that they live but a few years'[11] (p. 95). Cellini's statement has a direct bearing on the division of labour and the layout of the workshop alluded to earlier. Any craftsman who has tried to make a trumpet using historical techniques, and who has also tried for a brief time to set aside health and safety considerations, will know that this cannot be done in a pleasant work environment. The apprentice trumpet-maker, like any other apprentice, would begin in the workshop at a very early age and he would live and breathe brass until it was, literally, in his blood. In the heat of summer with the forge going full blast, the finely divided brass dust in the air would make the sweat run green from his hair. He would taste copper on his tongue for the first few months before he became insensitive to it, or 'brazed to it' to use a strikingly apposite Elizabethan phrase. The fumes from hot metals, particularly lead, mercury and traces of cadmium (of which they knew nothing) would contribute to all manner of unidentifiable ills. Even in the nineteenth century the chemical fall-out from the casting of brass was looked upon as merely an interesting phenomenon: 'The fumes which rise from the midst of the coloured fire are peculiar and penetrating, and the zinc eliminated from the molten brass falls in a metallic snowstorm, its flaky particles adhering to everything with which they come in contact' (Anon., *Boys' Book of Trades*, 109).

In addition to the poisonous atmosphere, the general workshop noise would certainly bring about some hearing deficit. The making, like the playing, could be a very noisy exercise and in no historical illustration of metalworkers is there ever a suggestion of hearing protection being worn.

---

[11] Theophilus gives the following instructions: 'Be very careful that you do not mill or apply gilding when you are hungry, because the fumes of mercury are very dangerous to an empty stomach and give rise to various sicknesses against which you must use zedoary and bayberry, pepper and garlic and wine' (p. 112). Agricola's remedy against lead poisoning during cupellation is for the workmen to eat butter whenever they feel hungry.

Hands daily blackened with metal dust and splashed with the liquors used to clean brass would become hard and cracked, and impossible to clean. The following is extracted from a report of 1760 given by a physician who attended a young man engaged in the brass wire drawing trade:

in drawing brass wire for the pin-makers, the frequent passing it through the fire, to anneal it, covers it with a crust, which it is necessary to take off [by] letting it lie for some time in the liquor . . . (which liquor is composed of water, oil of vitriol, alum, tartar, etc.)

When I first visited him, I found his hands quite stiff, and utterly incapable of any business whatever . . . the skin on the palms of them (the right hand rather the worst of the two) having the exact appearance of parchment, full of chaps; and when I endeavoured, by force, to streighten the fingers, the blood started from every joint of them. (Morton, 936)

An apothecary had apparently given him 'several doses of purging physic, but without success'. It is not implied by the above that working conditions were everywhere as bad, but it does make the point that there was much ignorance of the deleterious effects of chemical treatments and general workshop conditions.

Literally hundreds of instruments were produced by each family workshop every year but only a small proportion were made by a master trumpet-maker. It has already been pointed out that the name engraved on the bell garland would not, except in special cases, be that of the man who actually made the instrument. The continual ringing concussion of hammers on anvils throughout the working day and the poisonous fumes arising make it a virtual certainty that the master, the family patriarch with his name on the garland, would not be a regular visitor to the main shop floor. He would be obliged to serve his years of apprenticeship with all the rest, of course, and to excel, but his graduation from journeyman to master would almost certainly be a graduation to administration and special commissions. Parts would doubtless be made and rough finished for him on the shop floor, while in the comparative peace of his own workshop he assembled and finished the work. He might assign his best journeyman (his son or perhaps his nephew) to turn out pieces for him, or he might sort through a dozen bells from a military order to select one with the neatest solder seam and the most consistent thickness for his work. His hearing and the state of his lungs were far too important to expend upon tasks more fitted to a lowlier station. Baines's portrayal of the trumpet-maker engaged in 'arduous work over which [he] might have to work into the night, helped by his wife, to complete a large order of trumpets for a crowned head . . .' (*Brass Instruments*, 21) is touchingly romantic in view of what really went on in the workshop.

6

The Techniques

The type of work which modern technology is so succussful in reducing or even eliminating, is skilful, productive work of the human hands, in touch with real materials of one kind or another. In an advanced industrial society, such work has become exceedingly rare, and to make a decent living by doing such work has become virtually impossible.

E. F. Schumacher

Introduction

Chapters 2–5 have laid the groundwork for a description of the actual techniques of trumpet-making. One can now gain a historical and cultural perspective of the Nuremberg trumpet-makers, appreciate the diversity and complexity of their sources of raw materials, and understand to some extent their conditions of work and the kinds of tools they used. All of this is the very necessary background to the exploration of technique. It is now time to put all this together by following the construction of a trumpet from the sheet metal to the final twist of wire. As stated in the first chapter, perhaps the most efficient way of reconstructing early technique is to do it. No amount of theorizing upon the subject can quite rival a well-documented finished product.

The process of reconstruction requires not only close attention to the most appropriate techniques in their historical context, but also the use of authentic tools. In most cases the correct tools of the early trumpet-maker do not exist today, at least not in a form which would be the most immediately useful or appropriate. With the exception of files, which could hardly change over millenia (except in quality), most other tools must be adapted from modern brass-instrument-making tools or made from scratch. The maker of authentic trumpets must be a blacksmith and tool-maker of sorts as well. Hammer heads must be shaped and polished, the jaws of pliers must be ground to shape, and so on. Some tools like burins, punches, dies and mandrels are best made from raw stock. In addition, a simple home-made lathe on the seventeenth-century pattern is a nice addition to the workshop.

No two present-day makers will have assembled the same sets of tools, no matter how closely they might try to adhere to historical sources. The equipment described in this chapter is as authentic as possible, given the limitations of sources and evidence, but it should not be regarded as the last word. Similarly, the techniques described are based upon the best possible evidence, and examples of features on original instruments are used to illustrate and corroborate, but some details still need to be explored. In this chapter are illustrated the techniques which have proven to be the most efficient with the tools and materials available to the Nuremberg trumpet-maker. The most efficient techniques are, by extension, the most probable.

The Parts

The Bell

METAL THICKNESS

The bells of early trumpets and trombones are often of much thinner metal than those of the nineteenth and twentieth centuries. This has led to some speculation that bells were deliberately thinned during manufacture. It has been argued, for example, that, for reasons of resonance, once the bell of an instrument was completed, metal was removed by scraping to achieve the greatest thinness possible (Fischer, *Renaissance Sackbut*, 11).[1] While this deliberate thinning has been postulated only for the fabrication of trombone bells, there is no reason to assume that the techniques for making trombones were any different from those employed for trumpets. Indeed, the distinction between trumpet and trombone is quite artificial for the period when the metalworking techniques were first established. There are, however, good practical and technical reasons why deliberate thinning by scraping (or any other technique) would not have been done. If a craftsman requires a certain thickness in a finished product he will not work an over-thick piece of metal to shape and *then* remove material afterwards. The competent craftsman will quite simply begin with a smaller piece of metal in the first place, working it by hammering and burnishing to the requisite thickness. Scraping solely for the purpose of thinning is entirely unnecessary because it makes no sense to waste material which could otherwise be saved. Material was comparatively expensive; labour was comparatively cheap. In a simple application of William of Occam's much over-quoted razor, if experiment shows that any stage in the production of an artefact is superfluous, it is tolerably certain that that stage never originally existed. This having been said, it is quite likely that a scraper would be used on the bell, and other parts, to remove the black scale on the brass caused by heating, but very little metal would

---

[1] This information was derived by the author cited from the techniques of a modern maker—it is also used nowadays to make modern machine-made trombone bells resemble somewhat the earlier kind.

be removed in this process. The assumption of scraping to bring thickness down represents an inappropriate transfer of a modern technique to the historical context.

It had been possible long before the sixteenth century to produce an object like a trumpet or trombone bell with little or no loss in thickness during forming.[2] Metal-forming techniques of great sophistication were developed by the smiths of the Early Renaissance and it would not have been a difficult task for an experienced smith to work up a form which had an almost even thickness throughout. The trumpet-makers did not always do this. There are four possible explanations for the preference for thinned bells.

1. Tradition. The method of producing flared bells by thinning a sheet metal cone could pre-date the development of more robust techniques. The very evident conservatism of the Nuremberg smiths would enshrine the method long after it would otherwise have been superseded.

2. Economy. Strips of brass from the hammer mills were generally not very wide. Perhaps the use of a narrow cone for the bell was dictated simply by the cost or availability of wide, consistent strips. Labour for hammering metal was comparatively cheap, while good-quality material was comparatively expensive. Adding a gusset to give extra width would hardly serve because of the added inconvenience of fitting and soldering.

3. Expediency. It is far quicker to produce a bell by thinning from a cone than by wrapping and forming an oddly shaped piece.

4. Acoustics. Thinning the bell might have been regarded as enhancing the resonance of the instrument.

It may be that a combination of the first three factors decided the technique long before the resultant resonance became a factor. It is far more logical to assume that the physical process of manufacturing the shape had to be tackled *before* considerations of what the finished object might sound like. The manufacture of brass instruments in Nuremberg has its roots deep in the Middle Ages when, perhaps, forming techniques were not as sophisticated, and thinning a cone was simply the most efficient way to produce a bell. It is therefore debatable just what part acoustic performance of the metal played. Such later factors as the late seventeenth century development of wide garlands and heavy cast decorations, and the variety of thicknesses of base metal available in the eighteenth century, indicate that mass of metal *per se* might not have been as important as we think. If the resonance of thin

---

[2] For example, a detached tenor trombone bell by Oller of Stockholm in the Carl Claudius' Samling in Copenhagen shows virtually no thinning from the base thickness of the sheet to the edge of the bell. On the other hand, the bell of one of the most beautifully made brass instruments in existence, the tenor trombone by Georg Ehe of 1619 (Musée Instrumental du Conservatoire, Paris, E.754,C.660) is exceedingly thin. The bell of the Hainlein trombone in Frankfurt is reputed to be 0.18 mm thick *throughout its entire length*.

bell metal was indeed regarded as critical, why would such compromises have been made?

The degree to which the metal of the bell is thinned out is clearly related directly to the shape of the original flat piece—the less material used initially, the thinner the metal will have to become to achieve a given shape. In other words, a tightly formed cone using a narrow strip of brass will require more thinning by flaring than one made from a more generously proportioned piece. The process of thinning and flaring is more complex than would first appear. During hammering the metal spreads in all directions so that the bell expands outwards circumferentially, but also elongates. The ratio of circumferential expansion to longitudinal elongation is related directly to the shape of the hammer head and its area of impact. Clearly, for developing a cone into a flared bell, circumferential expansion is initially more important, but with a sharply flared bell the outer edges benefit from longitudinal expansion as well. A change of hammer head shape would be advantageous at this stage. Thickness of extant trumpet bells varies so much that it is clear no consistent approach to thinning was taken, neither were patterns and techniques between individual makers fully comparable.[3]

The shape of the cut-out piece of raw material is dictated by the degree of flare of the mandrel and the ultimate thinness required. Weigel's craftsman has five very narrow cones of metal (presumably bells) resting against the back wall of his workshop. They will be worked into shallow-flared bells like the one propped alongside them which, in turn, matches the mandrels on the wall.[4] These can be compared with the bell templates of the lady and gentleman in Martin Engelbrecht's illustration, although it is interesting to note that the bell mandrels and templates shown are incompatible; the comparatively shallow flare of the mandrel would certainly not require the use of a piece of brass with so much excess material at the wide end.

Due to the method of forming, the thickness of the bell is not constant around its circumference; it tends to be thicker at the seam and thinner on the opposite side, 180° away. This comes about as a natural result of forming a flat piece of metal with curved edges into a complex, three-dimensional shape. As can be seen in Fig. 43 (left), once the cut out sheet is wrapped and soldered, and before being hammered, its profile curves outwards on the seam side and is quite straight on the opposite side. Hammering the metal into a symmetrical bell (Fig. 43, right) causes more thinning on the side away from the seam than at the seam itself. However, this observation results more from modern reconstruction than observed data—measuring

---

[3] When Altenburg writes of various thicknesses of metal (*Versuch*, 10) it is not impossible that he is speaking of the degree of thinning of the bell, rather than the actual base thickness of the material, as it is the thickness of the bell metal which would contribute most to the player's perception.

[4] Even though the trumpet hanging up behind the craftsman is unlike anything that was ever made, its bell flare is more likely for the date of publication of the *Abbildung*.

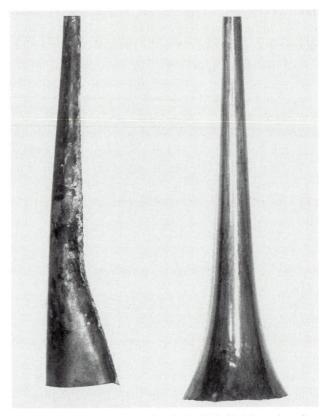

FIG. 43. The wrapped and soldered sheet for the bell (left). Note that the seam side has a curved profile, while the side opposite the seam is quite straight. On the right, the bell has been partially formed and has lost its lopsidedness. Hammering is confined to the first 6 or 8 cm. of the bell, regardless of the degree of flare required.

TABLE 5 *Thickness measurements of the bell of a trumpet by Hanns Hainlein of 1632, compared with a recent copy*

Point of measurement, clockwise facing bell	Hainlein, 1632 Thickness (mm.)		Copy, 1983 Thickness (mm.)	
	Edge of garland	2cms from edge	Edge of garland	2cms from edge
Beside seam (0°)	0.370	0.375	0.340	0.355
90°	0.350	0.360	0.270	0.330
180°	0.345	0.350	0.235	0.285
270°	0.350	0.360	0.265	0.320

Notes: The metal tends to be thickest at the seam and thinnest 180° away. In order to avoid measuring any inconsistencies at the seam itself, the seam measurement was offset to the side 5 mm.

the thickness of a trumpet bell at its extreme edge, with the garland in place, is nearly impossible. Table 5 shows a single set of measurements from a seventeenth-century instrument with a narrow garland, and equivalent measurements from a modern copy. These figures tend to support the above observation.

CONSTRUCTION

The seam of the trumpet bell, down to at least the position of the ball, is made from alternating overlapping tabs cut along one of the interlocking edges (Fig. 44). An extra 4 or 5 mm. is left along one edge to allow for this. Both edges of the sheet brass

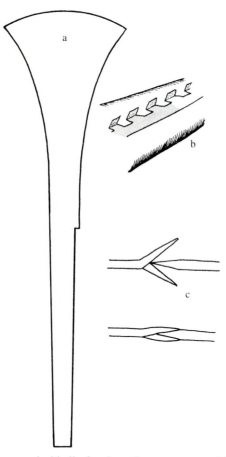

FIG. 44. The template for a typical bell of early 17th-cent. pattern (a). The details show the technique of overlapping the seam by cutting tabs in one edge (b), and a cross-section to show why it is necessary to file the edges of the metal into a knife edge before engaging the tabs (c)

must first be filed or scraped to a sharp profile so that the tabs interlock fully but do not add greatly to the overall thickness of the join. This kind of join is necessary where the metal is to be reheated and hammered many times. In most cases the seam of the bellpipe—i.e. the portion between the ball and the first garnish—only needs to be a simple butt join as it is not stressed after soldering. One does nevertheless occasionally see the toothed seam continued down the bellpipe.

To make the seam, the annealed metal is wrapped by hand until the tabs are engaged ,whereupon it is bound at intervals with iron wires. Once the tabs are engaged and the wires tightened, the whole seam is coated with borax flux, made into a thin, fluid paste with water. The seam is then hammered on an anvil to drive the tabs into each other and ensure that those on the inside are lying flat. The flux must be applied at this stage because it will not penetrate below the tabs once they are hammered down. Because the bell was very probably soldered 'in the fire', finely divided solder would be included in the flux mixture as suggested in Chapter 4, under 'Solders'. For soldering long, narrow objects like yards and bells, a long, trough-shaped forge bed is necessary, with tuyères from the bellows at regular intervals along the bottom. The bell is laid among the hot coals and covered with a perforated iron lid upon which more hot coals are heaped. The perforations at intervals in the cover allow the worker to check on progress. The coals are heated by pumping on the bellows until the flux around the seam is seen to turn very fluid and mobile, and the brass becomes brightly clean. This is the point at which the solder begins to flow. To maintain even heating along the seam, and to judge the point at which the solder had flowed evenly and completely, required great skill and experience. Fig. 45 shows a crudely made seam which has the advantage of showing the technique of construction rather well. Incidentally (but of interest to the present-day trumpet-maker) the modern propane torch works just as well as coals or blowpipe and incurs no detectable compromise in the finished product.[5]

Inappropriate solders and poor application were obviously points of concern in the early eighteenth century, as the *Handwerksordnung der Trompetenmacher* points out: 'In the fourth case, no one shall use bad hard solder, neither on tube nor bell of trumpet or trombone, out of which no good can come, upon fine of two gulden' (Wörthmüller, 'Die Nürnberger Trompeten- und Posaunenmacher', 284).[6] This

[5] Gary M. Stewart, Conservator of the Shrine to Music Museum, has pointed out that if an iron bowl with a central perforation was placed over the fire, the draught from the bellows would produce a vertical torch-like flame over which soldering could be done. Or a blowpipe might be used. The author did a great deal of this kind of work with a blowpipe and a hot coal held with tongs in the days when propane (or butane) torches were expensive luxuries. Whatever method might have been used, the author can attest at first hand to the skill and patience of the early soldering specialists. (Equally, the player of compromised instruments can attest to the skill and patience of the early trumpet specialists, without necessarily being obliged to follow their methods!)

[6] *Zum vierten soll hinfüro ihrer keiner weder rohr noch haupstück zu den trommeten oder posaunen gehörig mit schlechtem harten loth löthen, auss welchem nichts guts werden kan, bey straff zweyer gulden.*

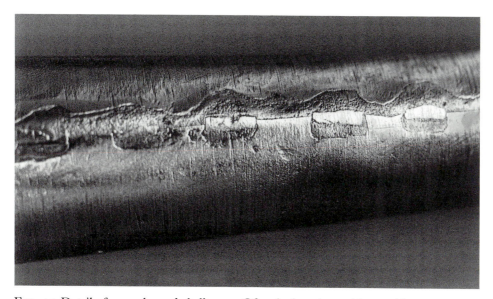

FIG. 45. Detail of a poorly made bell seam. Often bad workmanship provides an opportunity of elucidating technique; the overlapping technique of the tabs and the filling quality of the solder are both easily visible. (Georg Friederich Steinmetz, late 18th-cent., Musikhistorisk Museum og Carl Claudius' Samling, Copenhagen, No. X70)

concern could reflect the change-over from the traditional copper–silver alloys to alloys of copper and zinc as the latter metal became more common in the workshop.

Once the tabbed section of the seam is completed, the straight butt join of the bellpipe can be soldered. The edges are brought close together by burnishing them on a tapered steel mandrel with a heavy, polished steel rod. With the edges butted perfectly together the seam is scratched with a pointed tool to expose fresh, unoxidized metal and to leave a slight V-shaped groove along which the solder can flow. The seam is coated with borax flux, heated and soldered (this technique is dealt with in a little more detail under The Yards, below). At this stage the proto-bell is ready for shaping.

As pointed out in Chapter 3, brass work-hardens and therefore needs periodic annealing by heating to near red heat. It is critical to assess the point at which brass hardens fully during hammering because beyond this point the alloy becomes very brittle and it is easy to cause stress cracking. It takes some experience to detect the change in sound between the comparatively dull impact of soft metal, and the ringing concussion of hardened material. There is also a detectable increase in bounce of the hammer as the brass sheet work-hardens. Also, the hammer blows must always sound solid; rattling or bouncing of the bell indicates inefficient attack. The

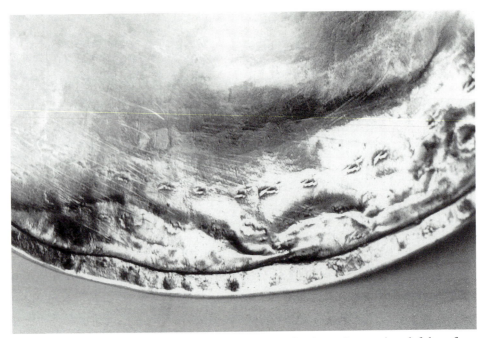

FIG. 46. In this detail of the interior of a bell, one can clearly see impressions left by a fragment of scrap metal (swarf) embedded in the horn of the anvil. This illustration is useful because it shows how the bell was rotated during striking, but it also shows how little attention was paid to basic workshop practice. (Cornelius Steinmetz, late 18th-cent., Collection of Ernst W. Buser, Biningen)

horn of the anvil should be filed smooth and then scraped before each bell is made. Fig. 46 shows how a defect on the anvil can become imprinted repeatedly into the inside of the bell if this is not done. Similarly, the hammer head should be highly polished and have rounded corners to avoid cutting the sheet. A small hammer of the same kind can be used to planish the surface, replacing the large welts with smaller and more evenly spaced ones.

The trumpet-maker in Weigel's illustration is holding the bell mouth away from his body with the bellpipe tucked under his right arm. It is actually a lot more comfortable and efficient to hold the bell in the opposite way, as shown in Fig. 47. In this way the exact point of contact of the hammer along the flare of the bell can be adjusted very accurately for the greatest effect. Hammering can either proceed concentrically, rotating the bell a few degrees at each strike with the left hand (as was obviously done on the bell in Fig. 46), or longitudinally, steepening the angle of the bell on the anvil a few degrees after each strike. The result of a spate of hammering, longitudinal or concentric, can be seen in a raised line or ring—the metal is

FIG. 47. The preferred way of holding the bell while hammering. The angle can be steepened simply by bending the elbow. Compare this stance with Weigel's trumpet-maker

thinned by squeezing between hammer and anvil, and can go nowhere but outwards. These rings or lines blend into each other as the whole surface is covered by hammer blows, and the bell therefore begins to flare outwards and extend (Fig. 48).

It is a common misconception that the entire bell down to the position of the ball must be hammered to shape. In fact only the last 6 or 7 cm. of most bells need hammering on the anvil (see Fig. 43, right)—the rest falls into place during burnishing, the next process. Nevertheless, while the widest end of the bell is being hammered to shape, the entire length of the tabbed seam also needs to be hammered well down to ensure that the tabs are fully flattened into each other. This can be done on one side of the bell mandrel, the other side being reserved for finishing operations, but a long thin anvil or stake would be more historically appropriate.

Depending upon the efficiency of hammering and the density of hammer blows on the surface, a typical bell of early seventeenth-century pattern may need annealing five or six times before flaring is judged complete. Annealing between cycles of hammering must be done carefully to avoid overheating the solder join. While most parts of the bell can be brought nearly to red heat, the seam must never get this hot. When annealing is done on a bed of coals, the seam must always face upwards so the solder is visible and heat comes from below.

Old brass had to be cooled quickly in order to keep impurities in solution; if allowed to cool slowly, annealing was not as effective. A trough of water was normally used, although the process of cooling could be combined with 'pickling' where

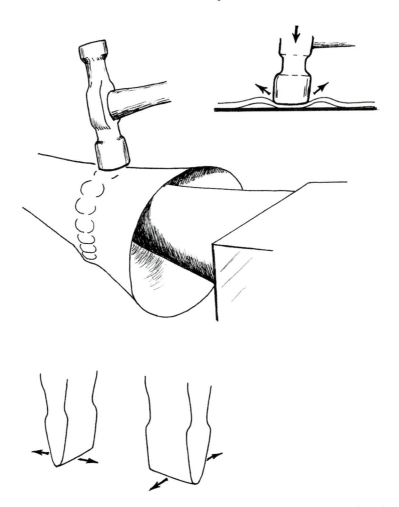

FIG. 48. The impact of the hammer thins the metal causing raising to take place (top). The raised ring formed by concentric hammering on the anvil is greatly exaggerated here for effect (middle). The shape of the hammer head and the angle at which it is used can cause the metal to flow in a chosen direction (below)

acidic solutions are used to clean scale from the metal. Solutions available included vinegar and salt, tartaric acid, sulphuric acid (vitriol), nitric and hydrochloric acids, and sodium bisulphite. Pickling is really only necessary just before final polishing.

During flaring, the bell is periodically tried on its mandrel in order to judge the points where it needs further working. (The black or brown oxide deposits from heating the bell transfer themselves to the mandrel when the bell is rotated in place,

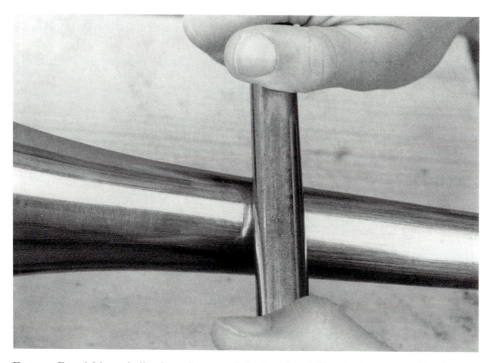

FIG. 49. Burnishing a bell using a heavy polished steel rod. Burnishing causes thinning and consequent spreading of the bell and removes hammer and file marks. Modern repairers use a range of burnishers with a gentle curves and comfortable handles, and some even come equipped with ball bearing rollers to eliminate rubbing while still applying pressure. The typical longitudinal marks left by the burnisher can be seen on the right

indicating the points of contact.) There is no way that consistent and accurate bells can be made by hammering alone. When a trumpet-maker was producing a set of instruments, it was essential that their dimensions were extremely close so that they all matched each other in acoustic response. The way to make reproducible shapes is to press the metal into close contact with a hard form of the exact internal dimensions. This is the function of the bell mandrel.

Once the rim of the bell has been expanded by hammering to almost the required diameter, burnishing on the mandrel can begin. The bell is slid on to the mandrel, which is well supported at both ends, and rubbed vigorously with a heavy polished steel burnisher, using as much weight as possible (Fig. 49). Periodically the bell is brought into firm contact with the mandrel by tapping with a wood or rawhide mallet on the end of the bellpipe. This causes some crumpling of the end, but it is left over-long to allow for this. The burnisher should be lubricated to avoid scratching;

tallow might have been used originally, although goldsmiths are reputed to have preferred saliva. Soap solution is equally effective and is more easily removable than tallow. Burnishing can be likened to hammering[7] in this case because squeezing of the metal between two unyielding surfaces causes thinning, although burnishing generally causes more elongation than hammering due to the direction of working. Where the brass is in close contact with the mandrel, the burnisher will continue the thinning process, but where contact is poor (as in the narrower portions which were not hammered) burnishing will press the metal into contact. Thus, during this process, the whole surface, both too wide and too narrow, is brought into close, accurate contact with the mandrel. Burnisher marks are often visible on finished instruments of indifferent quality, but hammer marks are almost always obliterated. Some filing is necessary during burnishing, particularly to remove excess solder, and it may also be necessary to do some filling with extra solder around small defects in the seam.

There are several possible ways of finishing the bell. Ideally, once burnishing is completed all hammer marks will have been removed and the surface will be smooth and polished, although still blackened from the fire. In actuality, there will be numerous small defects which defy eradication by burnishing. Of the techniques available, the most historically appropriate are filing, scraping, and abrasive polishing, in this order of effectiveness. The file can be used along the seam to remove excess solder and to thin down the overlapped tabs. Other deep defects can also be removed with the file, although with great caution in the thin areas. (If hammering and burnishing have proceeded well, such deep defects should not exist.) Scraping with a very hard steel blade will remove fire scale, flux residues, oxides, and even file marks. If the blade of the scraper is carefully ground, and if the scraper strokes are longitudinal, uninterrupted, and of even pressure, the bell may only need burnishing to bring up a high shine. One often sees finished trumpet bells in this state. Further polishing may be done with one of the many abrasive powders mentioned in Chapter 5, under 'Finishing Equipment'.

The bell mandrels in both the *Abbildung* illustration and the works by Engelbrecht have shanks projecting from their wide ends. As mentioned previously, these shanks were probably used for rotating the mandrel in a lathe with the bell in place on it for abrasive polishing (Fig. 50). Some instruments show characteristic concentric scratches which could have been caused by this process, although it is difficult to distinguish them from later polishing efforts done while the instrument was in use. These scratches should not be confused with the marks from spinning,

---

[7] The term 'burnishing' in this context involves deformation of the surface on a gross scale, but the distinction between burnishing and polishing is not as clear microscopically. An article by E. Rabinowicz in *Scientific American* (see the Bibliography) contains further information on the processes of burnishing and polishing.

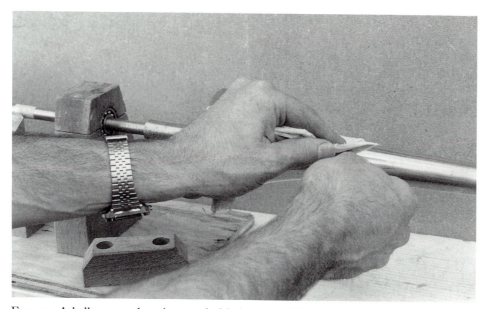

FIG. 50. A bell mounted on its mandrel being rotated in the lathe for polishing. A cloth soaked in abrasive and water mixture is rubbed firmly on the bell as it rotates. The large wheel lathe would be traditionally used for this. (This is clearly a posed photograph as the actual process is a lot messier)

where the rotating sheet metal is formed over a mandrel with a movable tool. Although a very old technique, spinning of trumpet bells only began to be applied in the eighteenth century. It was apparently only done sparingly in Nuremberg, but other centres practised it. Fig. 51 shows a detail of a trumpet bell where clear spinning marks are evident, which can be compared with the scratches caused by abrasion shown in Fig. 52. The interior of the bell can best be finished by using a small, curved scraper on a long wooden handle followed by a leather-covered wooden rod coated with abrasive. Pickling solution can be poured into the bell to clean further down.

As stated earlier, the sheet metal for the bell is always cut slightly too long because the narrow end becomes deformed as the bell is set on to the mandrel periodically with a mallet. Once the finishing work is completed, the bell can be cut to length. This is best done with a small saw, with the bellpipe mounted on a cut-off rod—a piece of surplus iron or wood of the exact internal diameter which prevents collapse or distortion of the still-soft brass while it is being sawn. In the finished instrument the narrow end of the bellpipe is covered with one of the three long garnishes. It is necessary to shrink down the end of the bellpipe slightly so that the

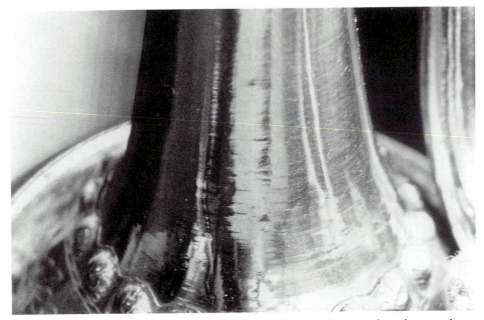

FIG. 51. Detail of a bell showing spinning marks. Unlike abrasive scratches, these marks resemble ripples, being softer and more pronounced. (Anton Kerner, Vienna, 1769, Trompetenmuseum Bad Säckingen, No. 11211)

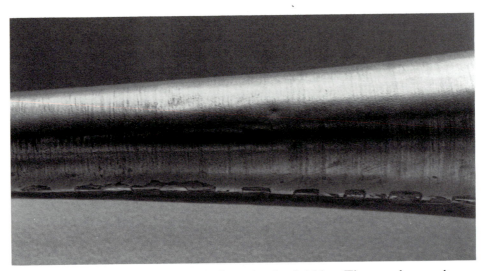

FIG. 52. Detail of a bell showing marks from abrasive finishing. The scratches are sharper and finer than those produced by spinning. (Georg Friedrich Steinmetz, late 18th-cent., Musikhistorisk Museum og Carl Claudius' Samling, Copenhagen, No. X70)

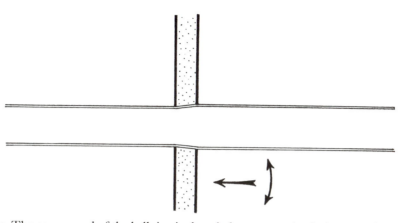

FIG. 53. The narrow end of the bellpipe is shrunk down to receive its long garnish by forcing it into a swage, a slightly tapered hole in a hardened steel plate. A little sideways movement aids the process. (The same process is used for all ends of tubes which lie under garnishes)

garnish will slip on. This can be done by gentle hammering on an undersized mandrel, or the end of the bellpipe can be filed down. The third, and most elegant, way of doing this is by forcing the tubing through a steel die, or swage, of the correct internal diameter to shrink it down (Fig. 53). Swaging in this way is probably a later development. (See also 'The Yards'.) When the garnish fits snugly on to the bellpipe, but stops short of its correct position by 4 or 5 mm., the bell may be considered finished.

The Bell Garland

Garlands vary a great deal in shape and size. In general, the earlier bells were thinned less and therefore needed only comparatively narrow garlands, while later ones required the extra support of a wide contoured piece of metal. Early seventeenth century garlands are conical in profile, as the difference between a narrow conical band and a shallowly flared bell is so minor as not to be significant. Garlands flared to match the profile of the bell came into use late in the seventeenth century.

Decoration also varies between the plain, utilitarian instruments and the elaborate presentation pieces (Figs. 54, 55, and 56). In the sixteenth and seventeenth centuries it was fashionable to cut the edge of the garland lying against the bell into points or darts resembling Classical acanthus leaves. Towards the beginning of the next century these were superseded by embossed scallopshells. The vogue for applying cast angel heads seems to have paralleled this. The instruments of the mid

FIG. 54. A decorative garland on a shallow-flared bell. There are six angel heads soldered on to this garland and the inscriptions are fitted in between them. (Sebastian Hainlein, 1657, Musikinstrumentensammlung der Stadt Basel, No. 1875.79)

to late eighteenth century often have little decoration around the edge of the garland except concentrically engraved rings.

Thus, although generally decorated and used as a site for the maker's name and date, the primary function of the bell garland is to provide support for the extremely thin metal of the bell. It has been suggested, though, that the garland (in trombones, at least) 'was made of very thin metal, attached only at the rim; it frequently stands slightly off the surface of the bell itself' (Fischer, *Renaissance Sackbut*, 11). Presumably this would provide free resonance of the thin metal below. On the contrary, the bell garland is always in intimate contact with the bell and is of the same base thickness. The finished bell is far too delicate to remain unsupported, and if the garland is not in close contact with the metal below, it clearly serves no purpose. No craftsman would attach a substantial 'strengthening' element, often embellished

FIG. 55. A decorative garland on an early 18th-cent. bell. There are four cast angel heads and embossed scallop shells. Note the misspelling of 'Haas'. (Johann Wilhelm Haas, *c.*1700, Musikhistorisk Museum og Carl Claudius' Samling, Copenhagen, No. F87)

FIG. 56. A plain garland on an 18th-cent. bell. Even though of about the same period as the Haas instrument in Fig. 55, it shows no decorative embellishment at all. (Johann Leonhard Ehe II, *c.*1700, Private Collection, West Germany, not numbered)

with heavy castings, to the thinnest edge of the bell and expect his customers to be satisfied once it tore off at the first sign of stress. The garland was closely attached in order to more than double the bell's thickness in its chief area of weakness. It was only in the nineteenth century that thicker machine-made and gussetted bells rendered the garland no longer structurally functional; until then it was no sciamorph. The assertion that the bell garland actually stands away from the bell may be derived from the very few poorly made late eighteenth century instruments where, to save time and cost, the garland is of conical section, rather than being flared to match the shape of the bell.

CONSTRUCTION

The simplest form of garland is taken from a crescent-shaped pattern (Fig. 57) which is wrapped into a truncated cone and butt-joined with hard solder. It is usually made from brass of the same base thickness as the rest of the instrument, although heavier sculpted examples are seen on the more decorative bells. An extra 4 or 5 mm. is allowed on the outer edge for turning over and crimping to the bell. A garland which needs to be contoured to match the profile of the bell is made in the same way, beginning with a cone which touches the bell at its top and bottom edges but is too wide in the middle. This cone is then placed on the mandrel used for forming the bell and is burnished inwards until it follows the contours exactly. It is periodically tested on the bell for fit, the difference between the bell and the mandrel (the thickness of the metal) not being significant. Once again, 4 or 5 mm. is allowed for crimping over (Fig. 58).

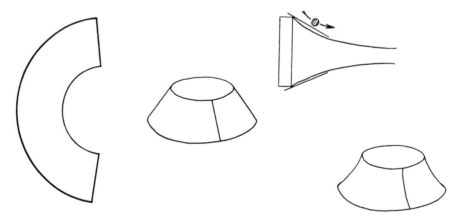

FIG. 57. The sheet metal for the garland of a simple 16th- or early 17th-cent. instrument is rolled into a truncated cone and soldered with a butt seam. If the garland must conform to the flare of the bell, it is burnished over the bell mandrel to compress its centre and flare its edges. Wider and more flared garlands might be hammered into shape before burnishing—note the hammer dents around the top edge of the garland shown in Fig. 56.

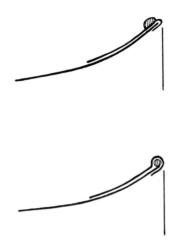

FIG. 58. Cross-sections of the traditonal Nuremberg method of attaching the garland by crimping over and using an attached bezel (top), compared with the late 18th-cent. technique, still used today, where a circular wire is trapped by the crimped edge (bottom). There are many other solutions to this problem visible on instruments from different periods and locations

MARKING OUT

The shaped garland is coated with a dark stain or pigment so that the layout of all engraving, embossing, cutting, and added pieces can be marked out. Engravers of book-plates and works of art used the smoke from a lamp flame or taper deposited on to a very diluted and almost-dry varnish. Perhaps the brass-workers did something similar. Nowadays a mixture of Prussian blue in shellac (called Engineers' Blue) can be used. The coating leaves a thin, opaque layer which can be scratched through with a sharp awl or scriber. In order to lay out a typical design, the garland is attached with screws to a wooden mandrel which can be rotated by hand. Concentric lines are scratched in first with an awl resting on a firm tool rest a little below the centre of rotation (Fig. 59). These lines provide the top and bottom rulings for the letters and decorative designs, which can now be laid out with the awl. Nuremberg instruments of the seventeenth century generally feature the maker's name, sometimes preceded by 'macht', followed by an abbreviation of Nuremberg, the maker's mark, and sometimes the date (Fig. 60). (Dated instruments tend to be the ones of better quality.) Judging by the uneven and occasionally cramped spacing one sees on some garlands, the maker often wrote the letters in free-hand, compressing or stretching the spaces as he worked around. The development of attached decorations and more room for engraving in the eighteenth century tended to give rise to wider variations on layout and design. Other decorative details may

FIG. 59. Concentric lines are scratched on the dark pigment with an awl or scriber. The garland is mounted on a wood mandrel in the lathe and turned by hand

be sketched in as necessary, although much work might be done with no pattern at all.

ENGRAVING

It is clear that some of the less accomplished engraving was done 'in house', but the finer work was probably contracted out to professional engravers who specialized in such work—the so-called *Trompeten- und Posaunenstecher*. The garland by Schnitzer shown in Fig. 61 shows specialized work of a very high calibre, while one by Hanns Hainlein (Fig. 62) is competent enough work, done very probably by the maker himself. Engraving is a daunting skill to learn as the control one needs comes only with long practice and many errors. The tools need to be exceptionally sharp and ground to very exact angles. Also, the angle of attack of the tool to the work is critical; if it is too steep the tool digs in and will not budge, if too shallow it can slip out and skid across the surface. It is therefore gratifying for the modern-day trumpet-maker to find the odd slip mark and mistake on even the finest trumpet bell garlands.

FIG. 60. Lettering and decorative details sketched out on a garland ready for engraving. There is no attempt at accuracy at this point—on some garlands it is evident that engraving was done free-hand, without even this much marking up

Two or three burins are needed for the standard 'in-house' quality of engraving (Fig. 63). Deep lines are cut with the wide-tipped tool and the finer cross-hatchings and shadings are done with either of the narrower ones. For the inexperienced engraver, it is often useful to do all the engraving with the finest tool, the 'knife', and then to chase the lines with the wider one. This cuts down on the frequency of slips. The garland should be mounted on its wood mandrel and the concentric lines engraved in the same way that they were scratched out originally. The tool must be held on a firm, angled rest a little below centre. When these lines are done the wooden mandrel can be attached to an angled base for working comfort when engraving the remaining work (Fig. 64).

There is a fine distinction between engraving and chasing. Where exceptionally deeply carved work is done, as on the highly decorated bell garlands, a hammer can be used to drive the burin or a chisel, thus carving deeper than is possible by hand pressure alone. Driving the burin with a hammer is quite unnecessary for the average engraving, but it is interesting to note that the engraver of the work shown in Fig. 10 (Chapter 2) did this, and did it in a hurry. The chatter and bounce of the

FIG. 61. The bell of a silver trumpet by Anton Schnitzer of 1581. This is very elaborate work of a very high calibre, more typical of the work of goldsmiths than trumpet-makers. Note the very deep engraving or chasing on the garland, probably done using a hammer and chisel. In places the garland has been pierced right through to reveal the metal of the bell below. (Kunsthistorisches Museum, Vienna, Sammlung alter Musikinstrumente, No. 248)

FIG. 62. Bell garland of a trumpet by Hanns Hainlein of 1632. The engraving is competently done but occasional slips can be seen. Note that two burins have been used for this work— a wide one for the outline of the lettering and a shallow one for the diagonal 'shading' (see also Fig. 64). The decoration on the darts has been formed with a punch. (Also visible is a flat metal strip, attached with a rivet, replacing the customary twisted wire through the garland.) (Münchener Stadtmuseum—Musikinstrumentenmuseum, No. 67/05)

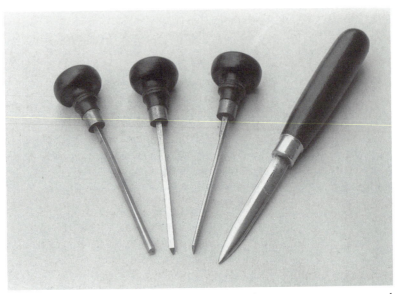

FIG. 63. Three burins are sufficient for the plain engraving seen on most trumpet bell garlands. Shown here are a knife, a medium cut, a wide cut, and a burnisher which can be used for rubbing out very minor slips

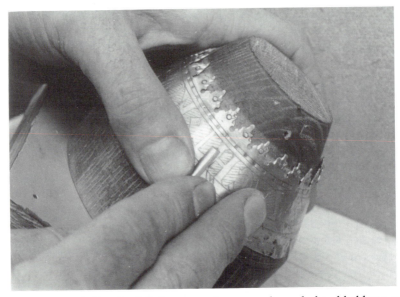

FIG. 64. Engraving a bell garland. It is mounted on a wood mandrel and held at a comfortable position on an angled base. In this illustration thin engraved lines are being chased with a wide tool to enhance them

tool are clearly evident in the roughly finished lettering. This is extremely degenerate work and is rather saddening. With a light hammer and good tools very smooth lines can be produced since striking with the hammer gives better control.

PIERCING

Occasionally the lettering on early garlands was cut out to reveal the metal of the bell underneath. This is generally only seen in the early bells where the metal was thick enough after forming not to be compromised (see Fig. 61). Each area of metal to be removed would be cut by a fine frame or piercing saw, working from a hole drilled in one corner of the piece (Fig. 65). The work is then finished with a range of fine files. The garland is hand held during piercing, while resting on a wood support, so as to give maximum freedom for cutting and filing curves and other intricate shapes. Blades would be very valuable items and used carefully to avoid breakage. Lubrication with beeswax or tallow extends their working life.

CASTINGS

Where such castings as angel heads were attached to the garland, a medium-melting-range solder would be used. The heat of the fire would be controlled so that the solder flowed beneath the castings while the garland seam remained intact. However, if the piece is pickled first to remove all traces of borax flux, the higher-melting-point solder will not readily flow if overheated. Also, the solder from the first stage can be coated thinly with lute (the fire clay used for grouting) or whiting, both of which prevent flowing. The undersides of the castings are shaped to fit the contour of the garland exactly in order to minimize the amount of solder necessary. Solder and flux mixture was applied over the whole surface of contact and the casting held in place by some form of clamp. U-shaped pieces of spring steel wire work well (Fig. 66).[8] Because the cast brass fittings are more massive than the thin sheet brass of the garland, soldering must be done with the whole assembly upside-down and not covered by coals. In this way the castings receive the most heat, which is then transmitted through the flux and solder to the sheet metal. If a solder with a low enough melting point was used (i.e. one with a base of lead and tin) a copper soldering iron might be used, rather than the fire.

EMBOSSING

Embossing on garlands is most often seen in the scallopshell motifs of eighteenth century instruments, particularly those of the Haas, but occasionally the decorative details on the darts were also punched, rather than engraved. There are two ways

---

[8] It is possible that castings were first attached to the back of the garland by hammering over small protrusions in their back surfaces, rather in the style of rivets.

FIG. 65. Piercing a bell garland using a thin-bladed jeweller's piercing saw. The piece is supported on a round wooden rod to give maximum flexibility when cutting intricate shapes

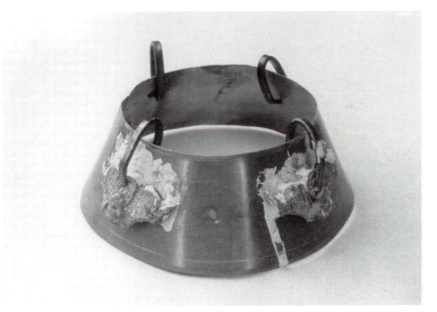

FIG. 66. Castings held in place for soldering with spring wires. Flux and solder mixture is applied liberally to the garland before springing the castings into place

of producing the embossed scallopshells. In cheaper instruments the features of the sea-shell were first punched from the front, with the garland resting on the anvil horn. The metal was then turned over and a round-headed punch used to raise the shell. For this the garland was rested on a block of lead so that the impact of the punch drove the brass outwards. This is clearly visible in an instrument where the bell has deteriorated to the extent that the garland is visible from below (Fig. 67). Scallop shells done this way are always spherical in cross-section and the embossed features are not always centred (Fig. 68). The second kind of embossed shell is of better quality. It was punched from the back into a lead block using a punch carved to the shape of the shell. This lends a much more sculptural quality to the embossing (Fig. 69). Finally, this second kind of embossing can be enhanced by chasing with a sharp chisel or engraving with a burin. In the better instruments the metal between the shells is often removed and their edges carefully filed and finished.

THE BEZEL

The outer edge of the trumpet bell is reinforced by a bezel which is soldered on to the garland. This is usually half-round in profile and has repeating designs punched and filed on it. A common design which requires only a simple punch is a repeating dart pattern (Fig. 70). Round brass rod of between 4 and 5 mm. diameter is annealed and pulled through a drawplate in much the same way that music wires were produced, except that a semicircular hole is used. The resulting half-round bezel wire is then annealed again and the patterns are embossed using a punch and hammer. Once the punching is completed the wire is very brittle and must be annealed once more. The work can be finished with a file, while small details can be engraved on to each dart. In spite of the above description, it is unlikely that bezel wire would have been made in the instrument-maker's workshop; it is evident that embossed wire of many patterns could be purchased (at least in the eighteenth century), as shown by the finely detailed repeating patterns favoured by some makers (Fig. 71). This would be produced by running a half-round wire through a rolling mill having specially shaped wheels.

The bezel must fit very exactly on to the garland; there is no allowance for error. First, it must be very flat on the back. This can be achieved by laying the finished piece face downwards into an iron form which has a semicircular depression drilled in it. The back can then be filed down to the level of the iron (Fig. 72). Next, it must be curved to match the curvature of the garland exactly. This is a compound curve in which the wire must be bent in two directions at the same time. It is periodically tried on the garland for fit. Lastly, it must be cut exactly to length and the ends hard-soldered together so that the join is invisible.

If the garland has cast decorations attached to it, fixing the bezel in place may be the third soldering operation. In order to avoid loosening of the castings or break-

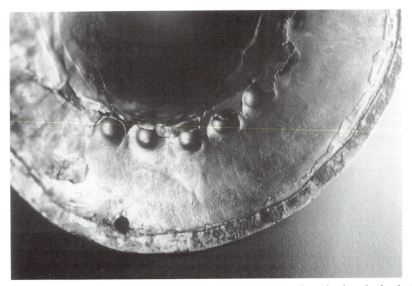

FIG. 67. This bell has cracked and parts have been lost, revealing the hemispherical embossings of the sea-shell ornaments on the underside of the garland. (Georg Friederich Steinmetz, late 18th cent., Musikhistorisk Museum og Carl Claudius' Samling, Copenhagen, No. X70)

FIG. 68. Embossed scallop shells on an instrument of indifferent quality. The shells have features embossed from the front and a spherical cross-section embossed from the rear. Note that in two places the embossing from the rear has failed to match that on the front. (J. W. Haas, *c.*1710–20, Shrine to Music Museum, Vermillion, No. 3601)

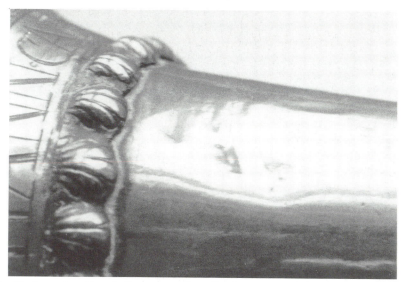

FIG. 69. Embossed scallop shells on a good quality instrument. The shell is embossed from the back and then engraved or chased to enhance its features. (Trombone bell, Johann Carl Kodisch, c.1700, Horniman Museum, London, No. 14.3.41–294)

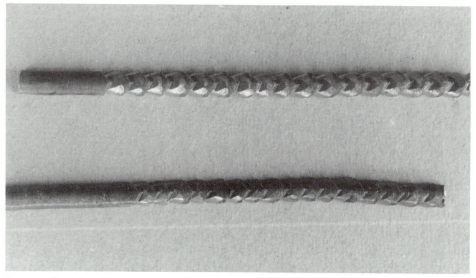

FIG. 70. Samples of bezel wire produced by punching and before finishing with a file. (Author's workshop)

FIG. 71. Detail of a machine-made bezel wire; the evenness indicates the use of contoured roller. (Note also the Nuremberg crest stamped on the garland.) (J. W. Haas, *c.*1690–1710, Shrine to Music Museum, Vermillion, No. 3600)

FIG. 72. The back of the bezel wire must be very flat. In this illustration the wire is placed in a half-round groove on a steel block and filed flat. (Photo: A. Barclay)

ing of the garland joint, a solder with a lower melting point must be used and the heat of the fire very carefully controlled. This is the true test of skill for the solderer. Once again, efficient pickling and a coating of lute or whiting can be advantageous. As with the attachment of the castings, the bezel can be held in place during soldering with U-shaped spring wires.

The order in which all the foregoing operations on the garland were carried out is uncertain, but it seems to make sense to do the engraving first, unencumbered by bulky castings or soldered bezel. Once the castings and bezel are attached, any solder which has flowed into the engraved lines can easily be chased out with a burin. Embossing may be done at any stage. The completed garland may be dipped into the pickling solution to remove excess flux and oxide and lightly polished with abrasive. It can then be considered finished.

The Yards

Seamless tubing was, of course, unheard of until fairly late in the Industrial Revolution, so all tubing had to be rolled by hand from flat sheet. The correct internal diameter of the tubing was arrived at by cutting the flat sheet so that its width represented the correct circumference, and then wrapping it on to a mandrel of the correct internal diameter. Nowadays one can calculate the width of sheet required by $2\pi r$, but the earlier craftsmanly way would be to bend a thin strip of brass around a mandrel and snip it gradually to length. Naturally, the established brass-instrument-maker's workshop would have patterns, perhaps generations old, already made. Ideally, the width of the flat sheet should fall short of the correct circumference by a fraction of a millimetre. This makes it necessary to force the finished tube on to the mandrel, causing it to become round and smooth in the process. The bore of Nuremberg trumpets varies somewhat over two hundred years or so, but no significant pattern emerges (see Table 1). For the yards a strip of brass about two feet (60 cm.) long is adequate, although the length depends, of course, upon the desired pitch of the finished instrument.

CONSTRUCTION

The maker of the tubing, assuming a division of labour, would first examine the cut pieces to make sure that any slight defects would appear on the inside of the finished tubing. Before any work was done the sheet would be annealed to nearly red heat and quenched in water. At this stage the alloy is so pliable that it can be formed around the mandrel by hand until the edges almost touch (Fig. 73). The mandrel is a true and parallel iron rod which is supported at both ends (it helps to grip one end in the bench vice and to support the other on a notched wood block). The metal is

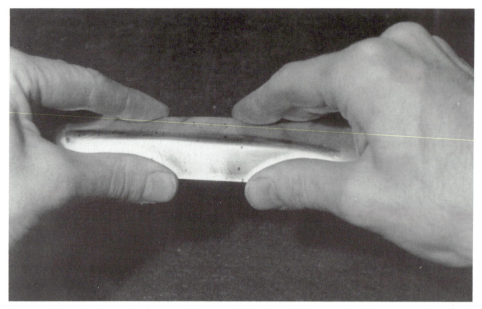

FIG. 73. Forming brass sheet around a mandrel by hand. The mandrel is supported at both ends and the annealed sheet is pressed around it

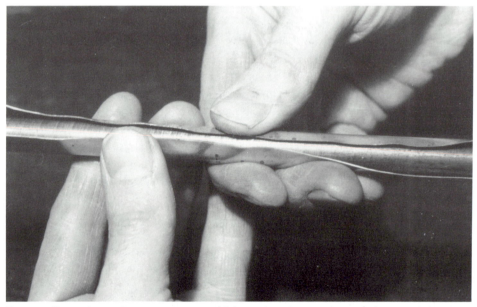

FIG. 74. Brass sheet of average trumpet thickness is soft enough to work around the sheet with the fingers. Light tapping with a wood or rawhide mallet can follow this process

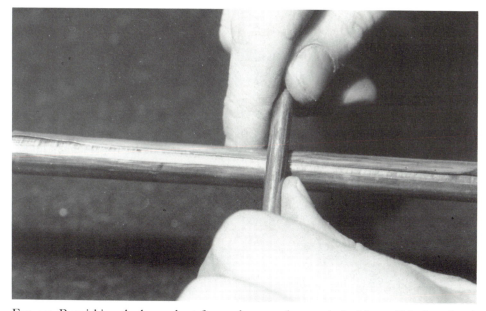

FIG. 75. Burnishing the brass sheet for a tube onto the mandrel with a polished steel rod. This ensures that the edges are straight and will align smoothly

wrapped around by hand and tapped with a small rawhide or wood mallet to bring the edges together (Fig. 74). The opposed edges are then burnished by rubbing longitudinally with a steel rod, pressing down on the mandrel in the process (Fig. 75). At this stage the tubing will be very nearly round and the edges almost together. In order to create an effective solder seam, the edges must be pressing against each other and exactly lined up. The way to achieve this is to remove the tube from the mandrel and squeeze it between the fingers so that one edge overlaps the other. The process is then reversed, the original under edge now lying on top. This puts a certain amount of spring into the brass, causing the edges to press on to each other when they are eventually approximated. It helps to pass a thin piece of brass strip along the seam in order to spring the edges apart and bring them into alignment. Once the edges are *exactly* aligned, with no detectable step, a sharp pointed blade is scraped down the seam to expose fresh metal and create a slight groove for the solder to follow (Fig. 76, left). As with all soldering processes, absolute cleanliness is essential; the exposure of bright metal ensures this. At this stage some trumpet-makers wrap iron wires around the tube to hold the edges together, but this does not seem to be necessary if the edges are sprung together sufficiently. Also, no matter how carefully the solder is applied, the wires can become stuck in place, requiring careful removal and occasionally causing damage.

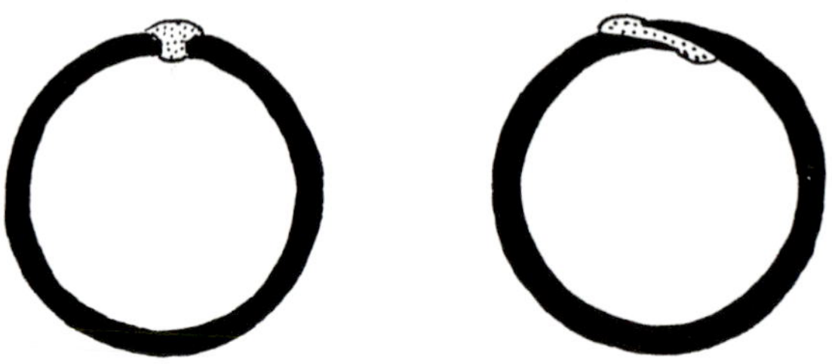

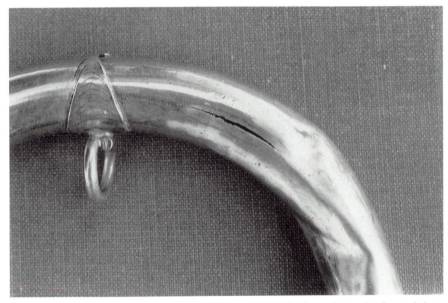

FIG. 76. Cross-sections of tubing showing the normal butt join favoured in Nuremberg (left) and an overlap join which is mechanically more sound, but time-consuming to produce (right)

FIG. 77. A failure of the solder on a butt seam—an example from the author's workshop. It is far better for this to occur in the workshop than later when the instrument is in use

It has been suggested that tubing seams were overlapped (Fig. 76, right). This would be the ideal technique as it provides a much greater surface area for the solder, although there is little evidence that it was ever done, at least until the nineteenth century. The technique of filing the edges of the sheet and forming it into an accurate cylinder were accessible to the early brass-instrument-makers, but were probably considered too much labour for a marginal return. It is interesting to note that failures of butt seams are not uncommon, especially when the tubing has been stressed (Fig. 77).

As with the bell seam, soldering would have been done in the coals. Flux and solder mixture would be applied to the seam before heating. Because silver solder generally has a very narrow melting range it is very fluid and will only flow along the finest of cracks. Some alloys are much better gap fillers, but do not flow so readily. Experience shows that for tubing seams a very fluid solder is preferable. The best general purpose silver solder contains 55 per cent silver, the remainder being around 10 per cent zinc and 35 per cent copper.[9]

Occasionally, small sections of the seam fail to unite, either because they have spread too far apart, or because the edges were not well cleaned, or because the flux may have failed. It is a waste of time to keep heating and applying more solder and flux; this usually results in the tube finding its way into the scrap box for recycling. The work must be cooled down, the seam thoroughly cleaned and closed, and then refluxed and reheated. Many feet of tubing must be made before joins can be soldered quickly and with confidence. Fig. 78 shows a seam which obviously gave its maker a lot of trouble.

HAND FINISHING

Once soldering is completed, the tubing must be replaced on the mandrel for finishing. If the tubing has been made slightly too small, considerable force will have to be used. The best way to achieve this without distortion of the still-soft brass is by placing the tube on to the end of a mandrel with a tapered end, then dropping the whole assembly on to the anvil, mandrel downwards. This forces the tubing over the mandrel by its own inertia. When five centimetres or so has been forced on, the portion of tubing in contact with the mandrel is burnished to smooth it out and expand it slightly, whereupon the process is continued. During this stage excess solder is filed off the seam, firstly by filing across at about 45° and then by 'draw filing' longitudinally. When the tube slides freely on the mandrel the seam can be finished by scraping lightly with a flat, sharp steel edge. The tube is then pickled to remove black scale and flux residues, and finally lightly burnished to a high shine with long, even strokes. This is the usual completed state of hand-finished tubing (Fig. 79). Fine instruments may have had their tubing polished with abrasive as well.

MECHANICAL FINISHING

Instruments of the second half of the eighteenth century show characteristic marks from drawing, or swaging (Fig. 79). In this process the tubing was made slightly over-size, and it therefore fitted relatively loosely on the mandrel. Excess solder was first removed from the newly soldered tube with a file, and the tube on its mandrel

---

[9] Slik Sil 106, available from MG Welding Products in the USA, can be recommended. A near-equivalent in the UK. is Easy-flo 55, available from Johnson Matthey Metals Limited.

FIG. 78. A poorly made seam showing excess solder and bad finishing. In view of Nuremberg's stringent quality controls, this sort of workmanship is surprising. (Georg Friederich Steinmetz, late 18th-cent., Musikhistorisk Museum og Carl Claudius' Samling, Copenhagen, No. X70)

was then pulled through a draw plate, or swage. A winch was used to pull the tube, liberally lubricated with grease, through the largest hole in the plate. A slightly smaller hole was used next, and so on until the tube was smoothed down tightly on to the mandrel. The difference in size of the holes in the drawplate should not be too great or tearing and distortion can result; 0.1 mm. increments work well, although this may be somewhat conservative. As with handmade yards, a light burnishing will cause slight expansion and free the tube from the mandrel. In both cases burnishing as the final process made the alloy harder and less prone to damage. The chattering marks resulting from drawing the metal through the swage are unmistakable (see Fig. 79).[10] The equipment is shown only by Engelbrecht and it can be assumed with some assurance that this was a new development of around 1750, or at least a new application to trumpet-making. The question of which technique is the most appropriate when making reproductions of Nuremberg instruments is answered by quality—very few of the mid to late eighteenth-century instruments are worth copying, and the few better-made ones appear to have had their tubes finished by hand in the traditional way.

To prepare the yards for receiving the long garnishes which fit over them, the ends may need to be swaged down even further as described in the 'The Bell' (see Fig. 53). Once this is done, and the ends are trimmed to length, the yard may be considered finished.

[10] But see Chapter 5, n. 9.

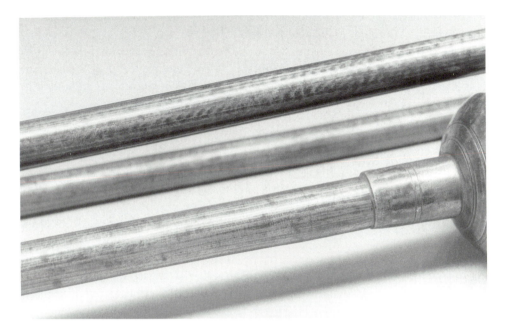

FIG. 79. An excellent example of both mechanical and hand finishing on one instrument. The recurring chatter patterns on the first yard (top) result from mechanical swaging of parallel tubing, while the marks on the tapered bellpipe (below) are caused by scraping followed by burnishing. (Lausmann, Graslitz, late 18th-cent., The Henry Meredith Collection, Arva, Ontario)

The Bows

Bows are not always semicircular; they sometimes have a compound shape, a flattened curve which begins fairly sharply, becomes shallower towards the middle, and curves sharply again. This form is seen at its most extreme in the slide bows of trombones where the shallow section is almost straight, although trumpets often have this form (see, for example, the second bow of the Haas trumpet in Fig. 9). The distance between centres of the bow only varies between about 7 and 8 cm. over several hundred years of manufacture, which indicates the desire to maintain the established classical form. The reason for the typical staggered placement of the long and short garnishes is not at all mysterious—once formed, both legs of the bow are cut to the same length. Thus, once the short garnish is slid over one leg of the bow, and the other leg is inserted into the long garnish attached to the adjacent yard (see 'Assembly' below) the familiar placement results. This may originally have been simply expedient, but the rigid adherence to the formula over centuries also indicates strongly conservative tendencies.

The tubing for the bows was made from the same stock as the yards, and on the same mandrel, although occasionally thicker material was used. In addition, one sometimes encounters instruments where the bow tubing appears slightly larger in diameter. It has been speculated that this was a deliberate choice of the maker, but as it is generally seen on instruments of poor quality it is more likely to be due to carelessness. There seems to be no acoustic reason for it.[11]

CONSTRUCTION

Two sections of tubing, each half the length of the yards,[12] are plugged at one end with hardwood dowels and filled with molten lead (Fig. 80). Diderot shows a horn being filled from the bell (perhaps with pitch), and Engelbrecht shows the equipment for melting and pouring. Air bubbles can become trapped in the tube causing it to collapse on bending. These can be detected by balancing the cooled tube at its centre; if it balances well, the lead is evenly distributed and it can be assumed that there are no large bubbles. There has been some debate over the acoustic effects on the finished instrument of using lead versus modern bending alloys (*Symposium*, 40), but this is entirely nonsense—the lead is removed completely after use and therefore contributes absolutely nothing to the piece of tubing which once enclosed it.

As mentioned in Chapter 5, there are several possible ways of bending lead-filled tubes and none of the contemporary illustrations throw much light on which was preferred. Perhaps the curious apparatus on the anvil block in Weigel's illustration is a bending jig, but it is uncertain. The simplest form of bending apparatus is a wood block with a radiused hole in it (Fig. 81). This is versatile enough to enable any shape of bend to be made with it, and it is simple to construct and use. A proper bending jig is not much more complicated; it can be made from hardwood with an accurately shaped profile of the bend attached to it (see Fig. 37). The lead-filled tubing is soft enough to permit bending to be done by hand quite easily. (As mentioned before, allowance is made for leverage during bending by making the tube for the bow half the length of the yards. The excess is cut off when the bow is finished.) While bending the lead-filled tube, the seam must be kept along the side so that it is neither compressed nor stretched. As bending progresses it is occasionally neces-

---

[11] Also, because lead shrinks considerably when cooling, it can sometimes be a loose fit in the tube, causing the cross-section of the bow to become elliptical on bending. A hasty measurement of the long axis might lead one to conclude that the tubing was actually of a larger diameter. Furthermore, because makers sometimes used a thicker stock for the bows in order to minimize wrinkling and to have material to file away in smoothing the inside of the curve, the outside diameter will be greater by the extra thickness of the metal stock.

[12] A one-foot length of tubing is somewhat wasteful as quite a lot is cut off both ends after forming, but one needs the leverage if bending by hand. The odd scraps may have been reused, perhaps for tuning bits, or recycled as scrap.

FIG. 80. Filling tubes with molten lead from a crucible. The tubes are clamped securely and their bottom ends are plugged with hardwood

FIG. 81. Bending a bow using a wood block with a radiused hole, the most versatile jig. (See also Fig. 37)

sary to hammer down any wrinkles which form on the inside of the curve. A hammer with a specially ground and polished curve on its head is used for this (Fig. 82).

During bending, the metal on the inside of the curve is compressed, while on the outside it is stretched. In fact, compression is minimal—thickness increases only slightly as wrinkles are tapped down—so most of the change in dimension is accounted for by stretching. This means that the metal of the outer curve becomes significantly thinner. In addition, disruption of the grain structure during stretching causes the metal to become harder while also creating a very granular texture on the surface, known as the 'orange peel' effect. This granular appearance, and the hammered texture on the inside of the bow, can both be minimized by burnishing. If one end of the burnisher is pivoted, a hand is left free to support the bow on the bench top or on a shaped block of wood. The device illustrated in Fig. 83 is a modern reconstruction using a universal joint to allow freedom of movement for the burnisher in all directions. This is by no means a new idea and it is certain that a similar means occurred to the early craftsman.[13] Prior to burnishing it may be necessary to file away excess solder.

All burnishing and polishing must be done with the lead still in the tube to avoid distortion and collapse. Burnishing is followed by abrasive polishing, which can be done by clamping the bow in a vice between wood blocks, and then applying liquid polish on a leather strap (Fig. 84). Once the bow is finished to a satisfactory state, the ends can be trimmed to the correct length with a small saw. It is advantageous to do this before melting out the lead for two reasons: the tubing can be sawn without distortion, and there is less lead to melt out of the bow with the ends removed. The lead can be melted out by wiring the bow to a fire brick and heating from below. Two small crucibles should be positioned to catch the molten lead. It is not advisable to heat the bow too much as any temper given to the brass by hammering and burnishing will be lost. It is therefore advisable to remove the piece from the heat as soon as all the lead has flowed out.[14]

Lead adheres hardly at all to brass in the absence of a flux, so melting will remove almost all of it from the bow. There are a number of compounds used by jewellers to prevent solder from flowing where it is not wanted, and any of these could be used on the interior of the tube to resist adhesion. As a final precaution, an iron wire is passed through the bow and used to pull a small wire brush around the curve. As with the yards, a garnish fits on to one end of each bow so these must be swaged down to receive them. (Swaging is illustrated in Fig. 53.) A light abrasive polish finishes the bows.

---

[13] Japanese paper restorers have for centuries pivoted the stirring sticks for their wheat starch paste vertically in exactly this way. Medieval flails use the same principle.

[14] Re-heating the tubing during melting of the lead, as opposed to a low melting point alloy, is the only conceivable way in which the acoustic characteristics could be changed, but this is surely just pointless hair-splitting.

FIG. 82. Hammering down wrinkles on the inside of a bow with a hammer with a radiused head. The bow is only partially formed at this stage. (Photo: A. Barclay)

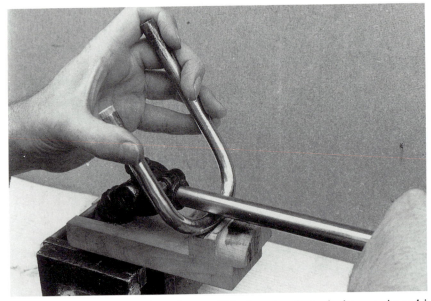

FIG. 83. A bow burnishing device using a polished steel rod attached to a universal joint. Both the outside and inside surfaces of the bow can be burnished by supporting it on the wood block in front. (Photo: A. Barclay)

FIG. 84. Polishing a bow with a leather strap dipped in abrasive polish. One end of the bow is clamped between wood blocks in the vice

The Garnishes

Although the general pattern of the trumpet evolved hardly at all between the sixteenth century and the close of the eighteenth, decorative details underwent several changes. This is seen in the variety of bell garlands, and can also be seen in at least six variations of garnish. Plain garnishes with no decoration at all were never used on Nuremberg instruments; there is always some decoration, even on the worst of the 'factory' models. The construction of garnishes is best illustrated by showing examples from extant instruments and examining their techniques of fabrication.[15] Discussion of the techiques begins with the most simple and concludes with the most complex, so the following six typical forms do not appear chronologically. Engraved rings, embossed rings, mechanically embossed patterns, cast, punched, and fluted decorations are all shown in Fig. 85.

The bodies of cylindrical garnishes are made in exactly the same way as the bows and yards. They are formed on a mandrel having the *outside* diameter of the other tubes so as to be a telescoping fit. Garnish tubing was probably made in long pieces and cut to length on a cut-off rod with a small saw as required. The long garnishes tend to be almost exactly twice the length of the short ones. It has been suggested that the longer the tube length of the trumpet, the longer in proportion are the individual garnishes, thus maintaining a very exalted aesthetic balance, but the evidence for this is far from certain. Perhaps it was done on the finest instruments, but among the run-of-the-mill material in museum collections no pattern emerges.[16]

ENGRAVED RINGS

The simplest form of garnish, having only engraved concentric rings, is normally seen on the cheapest trumpets, although three of the finest instruments of the eighteenth century by Johann Leonhard Ehe III have this form of decoration (see Fig. 12). A section of brass tube is placed on a mandrel which can be held between the centres of a lathe. The garnish is rotated and a sharply pointed turning tool is brought to bear on its surface (Fig. 86). The rings must be deep enough to be visible, but no so deep that the garnish is weakened. In this regard the angle of the cutting tool, or burin, is important; if the angle is too shallow, the engraved line will

---

[15] Herbert Heyde provides excellent details of garnishes (among other components) in plates 45 and 46 of *Trompeten, Posaunen, Tuben* (see Bibliography).

[16] The ratio of lengths also depends upon where one measures from. For example, the ratio of 1 : 2 holds true for the trumpet by Hanns Hainlein of 1636 (see Fig. 7) provided one excludes the length of the pointed darts. On even more elaborate work, such as that seen on the decorative Haas instruments, a standard measure of the exact length of the garnishes would be more difficult to make. Herbert Heyde provides a systematic analysis of the form and proportion of brass instruments in *Trompeten, Posaunen, Tuben*. He also gives extensive details of the metric system in use in Nuremberg in *Musikinstrumentenbau*, 74 (see Bibliography).

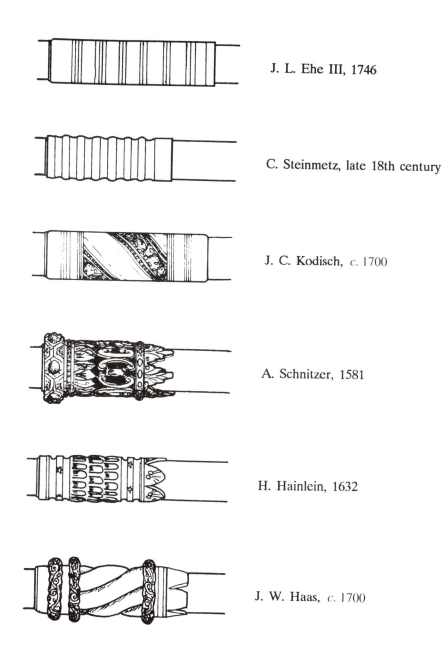

J. L. Ehe III, 1746

C. Steinmetz, late 18th century

J. C. Kodisch, *c.* 1700

A. Schnitzer, 1581

H. Hainlein, 1632

J. W. Haas, *c.* 1700

FIG. 85. The six styles discussed in the section on garnishes. They range here from the simplest to make at the top, to the most complex at the bottom

FIG. 86. Engraving rings on a garnish in the lathe. The tool is supported on a firm rest, slightly below centre. Note that the garnish is prevented from slipping by a wrapping of masking tape, a quite modern improvement. Originally, the metal would have been held in place by some kind of wedge. The piece can be rotated by hand or powered. (Photo: A. Barclay)

be too deep for its width. Sixty degrees is about right. While the garnish is being rotated, abrasive polishing can also be done to remove the burrs from the lines and to give an overall shine.

EMBOSSED RINGS

Engraving removes metal, while embossing merely rearranges it. Rings were embossed on garnishes by pressing a rounded and highly polished tool against the metal as it rotated on its mandrel (Fig. 87). The tool must be well lubricated with whatever comes to hand; quite probably the trumpet-maker of a few centuries ago did what is done today and used saliva, which is always in copious supply. The pressure of the rounded tool causes the brass to flow sideways, leaving a curved depression in the surface. This also causes the garnish to extend slightly in length. Quite often embossed rings were enhanced by interspersing them with engraved rings. A detail of a garnish decorated by alternate embossing and engraving of rings is shown in Fig. 88.

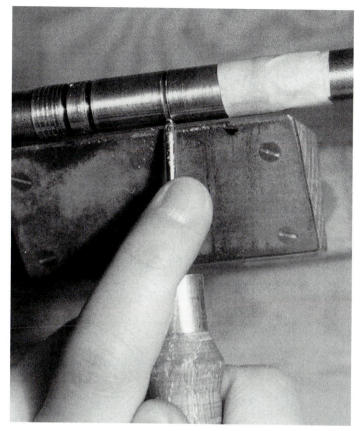

FIG. 87. Embossing rings into a garnish using a rounded steel tool. The tool is supported on a rest at the centre of the work and well lubricated. (Photo: A. Barclay)

FIG. 88. Embossed and engraved rings on a garnish. (Johann Wilhelm Haas, 18th cent., Adam Carse Collection, Horniman Museum, London, No. 14.5.47–244)

MECHANICALLY EMBOSSED

At the close of the seventeenth century strips of brass with embossed patterns came to be used by the trumpet-makers. Embossed patterns on sheet metal were no new idea (there is evidence of their use in the twelfth century[17]) but it appears that a technique of impressing crisp patterns on thick brass was newly developed. The vegetable motifs seen on garnishes of this period are typical (Fig. 89).[18] It seems that this material was available in long strips and needed only cutting, wrapping and soldering. Seams are always visible on this form of garnish as removal of excess solder by filing and burnishing would also remove embossed details. Engraved rings were almost always added to the ends of the tube.

CAST

Some garnishes are made entirely of cast brass. The delicately perforated features on the instrument by Schnitzer (see Fig. 61) are examples of this kind. As with all foundry castings, the work must be cleaned up with a file and lightly polished. Sometimes decorative features in the casting were chased to enhance them, or new features were added with an engraver. Little else needed to be done to castings before final assembly.

PUNCHED

Late sixteenth- and early seventeenth-century garnishes on ordinary instruments have designs punched between engraved and embossed concentric rings. The example shown in Fig. 90 is typical. It is likely that punches for designs like these were available from tool-makers who specialized in supplying the metal industry. The star-shaped punch was particularly popular. Punching is done with the garnish mounted on its mandrel and supported at both ends (Fig. 91).

FLUTED

Garnishes with helical fluting came into use on ceremonial instruments after about 1650 and by the beginning of the next century they had become the almost exclusive property of the Haas family (Fig. 92). As Baroque flamboyance went out of fashion in the last part of the eighteenth century, and as production techniques became cheapened, fancy flutings became obsolete. Fluted garnishes are produced by folding and wrapping sheet metal, but cast ones have also been found. Forming

[17] Cyril Stanley Smith illustrates his translation of Theophilus' *De Diversis Artibus* with examples of embossed decorations on an altar.

[18] Some flat cross-stays of early trombones have been replaced with tubular ones made of mechanically embossed brass. The tenor trombone by Anton Drewelwecz of 1595 (Germanisches Nationalmuseum, MI 167) is an example, which indicates a long working life for this instrument as the embossing is almost worn off with use.

F IG. 89. Detail of an embossed machine-made garnish. (Cornelius Steinmetz, late 18th cent., Ernst W. Buser, Biningen, not numbered)

F IG. 90. A garnish with embossed designs. Note also the beautifully made solder seams in both the garnish and the yard to which it is attached. (Anton Schnitzer, 1599, Musée Instrumental du Conservatoire Supérieur de Musique, Paris, No. E792, C595)

F IG. 91. Punching designs on a garnish. The piece is mounted on a mandrel to prevent collapse, and is supported at both ends

FIG. 92. An elaborate garnish with helical fluting made of folded sheet metal and soldered-on cast rings. This garnish is not of the highest quality; note the general poor finish, and how the fluting continues beyond the cast rings at both ends. (J. W. Haas, *c.*1710–20, Shrine to Music Museum, Vermillion, No. 3601)

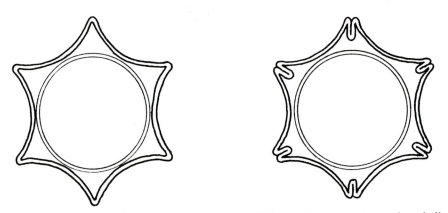

FIG. 93. Cross-sections of the two common ways of folding sheet brass to produce helical garnishes

from sheet is undoubtedly the original technique as foundry work mimics a form which would not normally be associated with casting. During restoration of a Haas trumpet from the Haags Gemeentemuseum the Brothers Thein discovered that both techniques had been used on the garnishes (Thein and Thein, 'Restaurierung der Haas-Trompete', 7) Perhaps during an earlier restoration or working repair a hopelessly damaged or lost garnish was replaced by a casting taken from a moulding of one of the remaining ones.

Two techniques of folding brass seem to have been favoured. In the first, sharp folds of approximately 90° alternate with shallow curves (Fig. 93, left), and in the second the sheet is pinched in upon itself between the shallow curves (Fig. 93, right). The first technique is obviously the simplest. Initially, the corrugated sheet for garnishes was prepared entirely by hand, in long sheets which could be cut to length as needed, but the later availability of preformed sheet should not be discounted. If embossed sheet and bezel wire were commonly produced *en masse*, then forming corrugated sheet mechnically would present no problems.

A sheet of brass slightly wider than the complete length of the garnish is scribed with diagonals of approximately 6 mm. spacing. The exact angle of the diagonal is important because this dictates the alignment of the helical flutes—once the sheet is wrapped around they must align correctly along the seam. Nor is it easy to calculate this angle as it depends upon the depth of curvature of the flutes and the sharpness of the angle of fold. Trial and error helps one to arrive at the correct degree of diagonal, and the extra width of the sheet allows a little lateral adjustment. An angle of 15° is about right. Obviously, any metalworker producing hundreds of these fittings would have templates at hand. The corrugations in the sheet are produced by gripping it between smooth, sharp-edged vice jaws exactly along the first scribed diagonal line, and folding at right angles. The brass is dressed down well by hammering a round steel rod of about 8 mm diameter on to it (Fig. 94). The next scribed line is gripped in the jaws and the process repeated. Lengths of corrugated sheet can be produced extremely quickly in this way.

For the more complicated foldings, the scribed lines are about 8 mm. apart to allow for the extra material pinched inwards (see Fig. 93, right). The piece is first folded at right angles along the first scribed line, then pinched to 180° in the jaws of the vice. With the piece still in the vice, the two sides are pulled apart and hammered down. Continuation of this process results in a long, flat sheet with pinched-up ridges (Fig. 95). The 8 mm. diameter rod is then hammered into the sheet between the ridges to produce the shallow curves in between.

The corrugated sheet produced by either of the above two methods must be wrapped around a mandrel of the outside diameter of the yards and bows. Cutting the piece to the exact circumference required is tricky, because it cannot be directly measured. It is best cut over-size and trimmed to fit exactly. Cutting should be done with a fine-bladed jeweller's saw rather than tinsnips to avoid crushing the fluting. While the piece is being cut to size the alignment of the flutes at the seam is also checked. Soldering is the same as with other components, although it helps to hold the piece together with iron wires, thus ensuring good alignment of the edges.

Both ends of the fluted section of the garnish must be made cylindrical so as to be a tight fit on the tube which the garnish covers. With the simply made flutings this is an easy task; it is merely necessary to place the garnish on its mandrel and hammer the flutings down concentrically at each end. The hammer head must have a very sharp edge to avoid blurring the distinction between the fluting and the cylin-

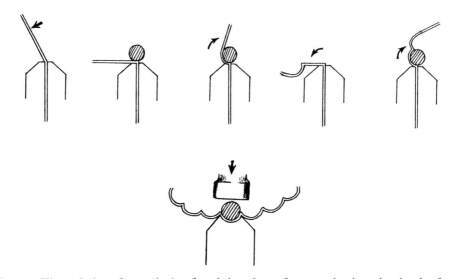

FIG. 94. The technique for producing fluted sheet brass for wrapping into the simpler form of garnish. The sheet is first folded at right angles in a vice and then bent into a shallow curve by wrapping around a steel rod. The process is repeated until as many folds are produced as required (top). The folded sheet is then laid on a steel block with a semi-circular groove in it, and tapped into contact with a steel rod (bottom)

FIG. 95. Fluted sheet for the more complicated garnishes is produced by first pinching folds in a vice (top), then tapping a steel rod between them to create the curve (bottom)

drical section. The hammer must also be wielded very accurately. Once both ends are hammered down they can be further reduced and straightened by forcing them into a hole in the swage plate. Because the fluted shape of the garnish gives great strength, it is quite possible to hammer these ends through the plate with a mallet. On the other hand, the flutings of more complicated construction (using the pinched sheet) cannot be hammered and swaged in this way; their ends must instead be trimmed off and butt joined to sections of cylindrical tubing with hard solder.

Each end of the fluted garnishes carries one or two cast brass rings which slip over the tubing and are hard-soldered in place. The cast ring on the 'open' end of the garnish is fitted flush with the end of the tube, while at the other end as much as 1.5 cm. of tubing projects beyond it. This surplus is usually cut into leaf or dart form and engraved and punched. As with all other components, pickling followed by light polishing completes the piece.

Saddles

A saddle with a wire loop is soldered to the inside curve of each bow. These loops were used for the attachment of the so-called banderole, or carrying cord, on ceremonial instruments, but were probably also used for tying the bows to each other to hold the instrument together while on horseback. Banners, on the other hand, were attached to the middle yard by tape ties or cords. Generally, the loops lie at right angles to the plane of the bows, but occasionally one encounters loops that lie in the same plane. The saddle itself is made of a flat piece of brass, usually of the same stock as the rest of the instrument, which wraps over half-way around the tube, the ends sometimes nearly touching. As this piece is held to the bow by soft solder, the more surface area for contact the better. The wire loop is hard-soldered to the centre of the saddle. Interestingly, the ends of the wire loop are always overlapped, rather than being soldered end to end (Fig. 96). The only practical reason for this is the added strength provided by a greater soldering surface, although it is probably another of those small details which were retained for generations by tradition.

CONSTRUCTION

The pieces for the saddle are small enough to be cut from the scrap brass left over from cutting the curved shape of the bell. As usual, the unblemished side is chosen to lie on the outside. A variety of engraved patterns can be found on saddles, the most common being the so-called 'rockered' design seen in Fig. 96. Engraving is best done before the piece is bent into shape and soldered. Indeed, it makes a lot of sense to engrave a dozen or so saddles on to scrap pieces of brass before even cut-

Fɪɢ. 96. Detail of a saddle. The ends of the wire loop are placed alongside each other rather than joining end to end. Note that the wrinkles formed when bending the bow have not been completely removed. (J. W. Haas, *c.*1710–20, Shrine to Music Museum, Vermillion, No. 3601)

ting them out; there is more material to hold on to. Otherwise, individual pieces can be pressed into a block of warm pitch or sealing wax to stick them in place while engraving.

The shaped and engraved piece is wrapped around a mandrel of the outside diameter of the tubing. It is essential to do this before the loop is soldered on, otherwise a flat spot will occur where the thickness of the solder prevents smooth bending. The loop is made of brass wire, about 1 mm. in diameter, which is formed around a steel rod of about 6 mm. diameter. These measurements are quite consistent among Nuremberg instruments. The same hard solder used for the rest of the instrument is used for attaching the loop, and it is here on such fine details that a blowpipe and glowing coal prove far superior to soldering in the hearth.

The saddle with the loop attached is pickled to remove flux and oxides, and excess solder is filed away if necessary. Engraving which may have become filled with solder is chased out and the completed piece lightly abrasive polished.

The Ball

The ball began as a fairly small protuberance, probably derived from oriental models and originally covering a joint between the bell and bellpipe, and grew to be the

FIG. 97. A ball formed from two hemispheres of sheet metal soldered at their edges. In this instrument the ball is mounted on a machine-embossed sleeve. (Cornelius Steinmetz, late 18th cent., Ernst W. Buser, Biningen, not numbered)

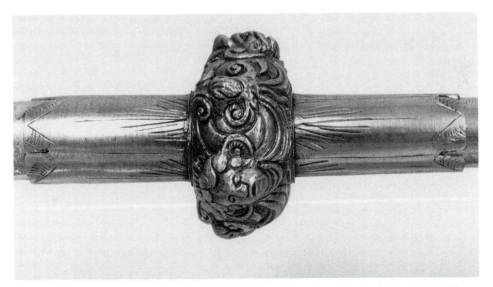

FIG. 98. A ball made from a casting soldered onto a sheet metal sleeve. (J. W. Haas, c.1710–20, Shrine to Music Museum, Vermillion, No. 3601)

substantial feature of the eighteenth-century instruments. It is mounted on a sleeve or garnish of brass tubing tapered to fit tightly at the correct place on the bell. Decorative features on the sleeve follow the pattern of the garnishes. In most cases the ball is made of hammered sheet brass (Fig. 97), although castings were used on decorative instruments, particularly by the Haas in the eighteenth century (Fig. 98). Hammered sheet balls often carry engraved concentric rings and sometimes further free-hand engraving. For example, the balls of a pair of trumpets by Johann Carl Kodisch (Germanisches Nationalmuseum, MIR 162 and 163) are richly decorated with floral motifs enclosed by concentric lines. Occasionally slits are cut into the ball with a saw.

CONSTRUCTION

The sheet metal ball was formed in two halves by hammering fairly thick brass (approximately 1 mm.) into a concave steel form called a dapping block. A hammer with a long, thin head and a rounded tip can be used for this, or a dapping punch, the male counterpart of the block, can be used. This is exactly the technique which Jost Amman illustrates for the thimble-maker in the *Ständebuch* of 1568 (Fig. 99). Thick sheet is chosen for four reasons: it is easier to hammer evenly into the depression without wrinkling at the edges, it does not become too thin on stretching, it is easier to solder thick hemispheres together at their edges, and much metal can be removed when truing up the ball without fear of thinning or breaking through. When two half balls have been made by hammering brass into a dapping block, the surplus material is trimmed off with tinsnips and the edges filed flat. The halves are then clamped together and hard-soldered to each other.

The ball must be mounted concentrically on its sleeve, so it is necessary to drill the holes in both sides very accurately. This is best done on a lathe, gripping the ball gently at its edges and slowly opening out the holes with a small, hooked turning tool. Nowadays it is fairly easy to grip an object like a hollow ball in a lathe chuck, but in earlier times it would have had to be cemented with pitch or sealing wax on to a wooden arbor which could be mounted in the headstock. When the holes are opened out to the correct diameter—one is slightly larger than the other due to the taper—the ball can be hard-soldered to its sleeve. (The sleeve is made and finished in the same way as the garnishes, except that it is mounted on a tapered mandrel for concentric engraving or embossing as required.) It is advisable to drill two or three holes of about 4 mm. diameter through the sleeve below the place where the ball will lie; this ensures that the hollow interior of the ball can be flushed out with pickling solution. It has been noted that some balls are mounted not on one sleeve, but two short sections, thus leaving the interior even more open for cleaning (Smithers, *Baroque Trumpet*, 74).

FIG. 99. The Thimble-maker from the *Ständebuch* of Jost Amman and Hans Sachs (1568). The technique of making thimbles by pounding brass sheet into a dapping block is exactly the same as that used for producing the two halves of the trumpet ball

The ball and its sleeve are next mounted on a tapered mandrel and returned to the lathe for truing. Because the ball is made from thick metal, an ordinary hand-held turning tool can be used to shape it. Light burnishing with a flat steel tool followed by abrasive polishing will complete the ball unless further engraving, either in the lathe or free-hand, is called for.

Assembly

When silver and gold plate are required on individual fittings, this is done before assembly. Plating was done almost exclusively by amalgam, using either silver or gold in mercury (see Chapter 5, under 'Gilding').

A characteristic of brass instruments made before the nineteenth century is their ease of dismantling without tools for cleaning and repair. On trumpets all joints are tapered sockets where the component nearest to the mouthpiece is inserted into the following component. To do this with tubing of the same size throughout, one end must be expanded and the other contracted. There are four such joints on the natural trumpet, all located in the region of the bows, and all are covered by garnishes. In addition, the receiver is also expanded to accept the mouthpiece shank.

Before tapering any joints, the long garnishes must be slipped into place on the yards and the short ones on to the bows. The ends of the yards and bows were already swaged down so that the garnishes became a smooth but firm fit, stopping some 4 or 5 mm. short of their correct positions (see Fig. 53). A wood or rawhide mallet is used to set the garnishes securely in place. The seams, where visible, are positioned so as to be unobtrusive when the instrument is assembled. For example, the seams of the bow garnishes usually lie along the inside of the bow, while the yards are rotated so that the seams of their garnishes also face inwards.

With a garnish overlying the end of the tube, its thickness is now at least doubled, and expansion of the interior can proceed without fear of damage (the seams are especially prone to splitting). A good tool for expansion is a square steel reamer with a taper of about 1° which has two functions: it causes the metal to stretch as it is rotated on it, and also thins the inner tube by abrasion (Fig. 100). In original instruments where the garnishes have become removable it is possible to see how the inner tube has been thinned by this process. No solder was ever used to attach garnishes; expansion of the inner tubing causes them to seize in place. The interior is expanded to the outside diameter of the tubing, an increase of a little under 1 mm. with average thickness of metal. The same tool is used for expanding the mouthpiece receiver, the opening being checked occasionally with a standard taper with increments marked on it. The opening is in the order of 11.5 to 12 mm. in diameter and a 'standard' mouthpiece should fit half-way in.[19]

The ends of the yards and bows must be swaged down to fit into their opposite numbers. This is done by tapping or forcing the tube into a tapered hole in a block of steel, the taper being the same as that on the garnish reamer (Fig. 101). It helps to have the tubing mounted on its mandrel for this operation. One end of the mandrel is tapered to allow for the shrinking of the tube. The tubing must be shrunk down a little under 1 mm., corresponding to the amount of expansion under the garnishes. The components are periodically tried in each other for fit. For a secure joint, the inner tube must fit into the outer to a depth of at least the diameter of the tubes. It is often fitted further than this. (When trimming the yards this extra length will have been allowed for.) A secure and airtight fit is ensured by grinding the two components into each other with any fine abrasive mixed with water. The end of

---

[19] Standard tapers and dimensions appear to have been first adopted in the latter half of the 17th century; Smithers points out the military advantages of standard, interchangeable components (*Baroque Trumpet*, 337).

FIG. 100. Using a tapered square tool to ream out the end of a bow to receive the tapered end of the yard. This process expands the tubing into the garnish but also removes some metal from the inside by scraping. (Photo: A. Barclay)

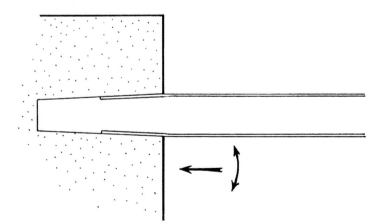

FIG. 101. The tubes which fit under the garnishes are shrunk down by forcing them into a tapered hole in a steel block. This is not a true swage as it is not open-ended. A little sideways movement during forcing aids the shrinking process

the bellpipe has a long garnish attached and expanded out in the same way as the yards.

The garland is attached to the bell solely by turning its edge and crimping it down (see Fig. 58). The neatness with which this is done is the key to the quality of the instrument (Fig. 102) although even the finest instruments show the odd wrinkle or inconsistency. With the garland placed on the bell, its edge is gripped in the jaws of a pair of wide, flat pliers. Soft jaws of brass or copper prevent the metal from being scratched. The edge is bent a few degrees inwards and the pliers are then moved along a little less than their width and this slight bending repeated, until a full circle of the garland has been accomplished. With the next circuit the bend inwards is increased slightly, and so on until the rim is bent at such an angle that the handles of the pliers touch the other side of the bell (Fig. 103). Clearly, bending the metal inwards causes its diameter to decrease, so ripples or wrinkles will rise as the metal tries to accommodate to this. Slow, incremetal bending and great care in lining up the jaws of the pliers will ensure that the rim remains smooth and even, and that the brass sheet is compressed into shape. With the garland rim folded over as far as is possible with the pliers, any small wrinkles which may still have formed are hammered out on a stake shaped to the inside of the bell. If the edge is well dressed down at this stage, neatness of the finished job is assured. The final turning of the rim is done by hammering from the inside with the edge of the bell, just above the bezel, resting in a groove on the sharp edge of an anvil or stake. A small, light ham-

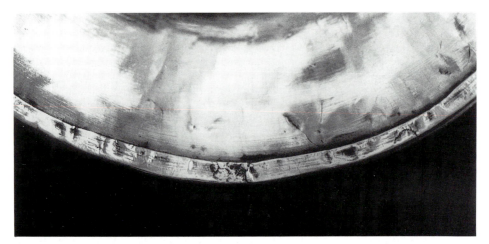

FIG. 102. When turning the garland rim, and crimping it down hurriedly onto the edge of the bell, wrinkles often form. These are even seen on the finest instruments. However, garlands are removed and replaced during repair and restoration, so some caution should be used before criticizing workmanship. (Johann Leonhard Ehe II, 18th cent., Private Collection, West Germany, not numbered)

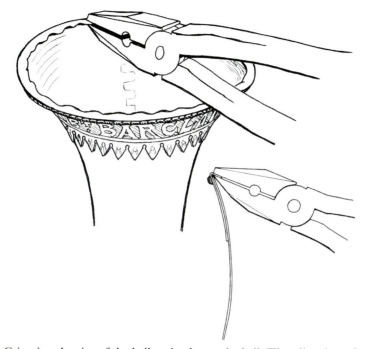

FIG. 103. Crimping the rim of the bell garland over the bell. The pliers have flat, polished faces and one jaw is ground to a wedge-shape. Obviously, crimping with the pliers can only go as far as the handles of the pliers will allow

mer with a slightly rounded head is used for this (Fig. 104). At this stage the metal has folded beyond a right angle and is now being stretched back to nearly its original circumference, so further wrinkling is not to be expected. Before final crimping down the seam of the bell is carefully aligned with the seam in the garland.

The ball is friction-fitted more or less midway along the bell. The term 'more or less' is used advisedly as the position of the ball, like other features of the classic trumpet, has been argued to be calculated upon the Golden Mean, an aesthetic construction of the Renaissance which seeks to explain and dictate form and balance. If all balls on all extant trumpets were similarly placed, this theory might have a little more validity, although there is clearly a 'right' position.

Balls on original instruments are sometimes immovable, but it appears that the ball sleeve, like all the other joints on the trumpet, was never originally soldered in place. In fact, the only solder joins made to the instrument during final assembly are where the saddles are joined to the bows. The saddle is coated with flux and held in place with wire, and a low melting point solder applied to secure it in the centre of the bow, facing inwards.

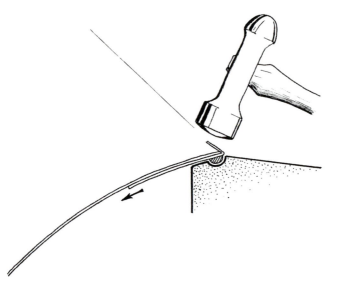

FIG. 104. Hammering the turned edge of the garland over. The edge of the garland is laid on a stake with a semi-circular depression in its top surface. The bezel is hooked into this depression and the bell pulled in the direction of the arrow while hammering. This ensures a tight fit for the garland and prevents the thin edge of the bell from being crumpled. A light hammer with a rounded and polished head is used for tapping the rim down

A wooden spacer block, held in place with tapes and cords, is traditionally used to secure the bellpipe to the mouthpipe. This method of making the instrument rigid was in use from at least the middle of the seventeenth century. It has been suggested that a removable wood block was favoured over (for example) soldered stays for acoustic reasons, but it is surely more likely to be due to its ease of dismantling.[20] The mouthpipe normally lies to the right of the bellpipe from the player's perspective. Oak seems to be the preferred wood for the block, for no clearly accountable reason. It is made a little thicker than the diameter of the tubing and has semicircular grooves cut in opposite edges to accommodate the bellpipe and mouthpipe. It is often slightly tapered along its length so that the tubes do not lie parallel to each other, but converge towards the mouthpiece. There is no prescribed method of tying the block in place. This author prefers to first bind the block around with linen tape, pulled extremely tightly, before applying the decorative cord in the manner shown in Fig. 105.

[20] Quite a number of Nuremberg instruments have had soldered stays added (see e.g. the instrument in Fig. 13 by Wittmann) but no evidence for their detrimental effect has been noted. An acoustic argument has also been put forward to account for the loose flat stays on early trombone slides. Again, ease of dismantling, and especially ease of alignment of handmade tubing, are more probable explanations.

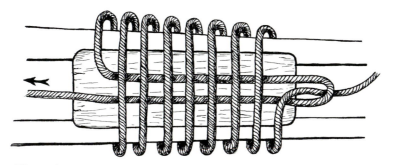

FIG. 105. The technique for binding the block to the bellpipe and first yard. There are, of course, many ways of tying the cords, this being one of the neatest and most convenient if no tasselled ends are required

With the block in place the front bow either touches the bell garland or lies very close to it. As the bow obviously obscures parts of the decoration of the garland, the seams of both the bell and the garland are positioned to coincide. This usually places the maker's name in the most advantageous position. To further secure the instrument, a thin wire (approximately 0.4 mm. in diameter) is passed through a hole drilled through the garland and bell, and wrapped around the saddle on the inside of the bow. Although it is best to drill this hole, the raised edges around the holes on some examples indicate that they were sometimes punched through. This curiously crude method of securing is often replaced by something more permanent, although hardly more elegant (see, for example, Fig. 62), but it is obviously the most expedient for rapid dismantling and reassembly. With this final twist of wire the trumpet is finished. Fig. 106 shows two completed instruments from the author's workshop.

Accessories

Shanks and Crooks

A trumpet for anything but basic field use would be supplied with tuning shanks (or bits) and crooks, making it playable in other keys. Instruments were probably made slightly sharp, so a set of perhaps three short shanks might be supplied. In addition, an instrument in D might also be supplied with coiled crooks for C sharp and C, and perhaps other lower pitches as well (Fig. 107). Few trumpet shanks or crooks definitely from Nuremberg survive from the seventeenth and eighteenth centuries.

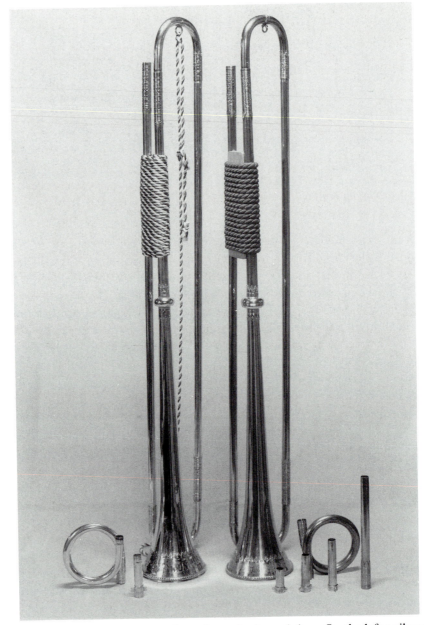

FIG. 106. Two completed trumpets from the author's workshop. On the left a silver- and gold-plated instrument made under the author's direction by Thomas Strang; and on the right a brass instrument after Hanns Hainlein of 1632, with tuning bits, shank, and crook. (Photo: C. Bigras)

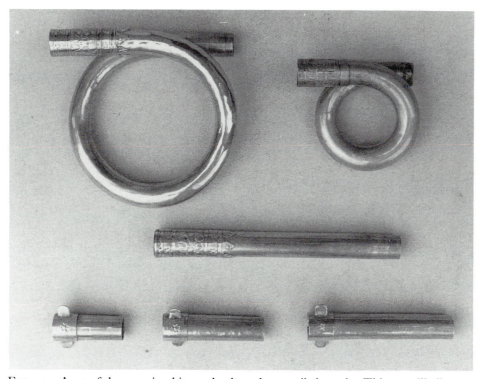

FIG. 107. A set of three tuning bits, a shank, and two coiled crooks. This set will allow an instrument pitched in modern D (A=440Hz) to be played in Baroque D (A=415Hz), modern C, and Baroque C, and also allow fine tuning of any of these

Shanks are made from tubing of the same diameter as the yard and bows.[21] The receiver is reamed out to accept the mouthpiece taper, and the opposite end is swaged down to be a firm fit in the receiver of the instrument. A short garnish would be fixed over the receiver for both strengthening and appearance. Most nineteenth century shanks also have small 'ears' soldered on to opposite sides of the garnish for assisting removal, and this was doubtless not a new idea.

Crooks are also made of standard-diameter tubing and are formed in the same way as the bows. A jig with a circular form mounted on it enables the crook to be bent a full 360° (see Fig. 37). As with the shanks, one end of the crook carries a small garnish over the tapered receiver, and the other is swaged down to fit into the instrument.

---

[21] Crooks and shanks of a narrower diameter are sometimes supplied today, but there is little historical basis for this.

Mouthpieces

From the seventeenth century onwards mouthpieces were customarily made from brass castings which were finish-turned in the lathe and reamed out with tapered tools. Turning of these castings would be done by hand, probably on the pole lathe described in Chapter 5, and the profile would be checked with an intricate metal template. As machining methods became more sophisticated, the whole outer form of the mouthpiece could be formed on the lathe in one stroke with a cutting tool shaped to the exact profile. Joseph Moxon (1703) refers to a method of cutting profiles in moulding in this way.

Before whole castings became generally available mouthpieces were either made up from sheet stock or had a cast cup attached to a rolled tubular shank. The two trumpets of 1578 by Jacob Steiger of Basle (now in the Historisches Museum, Basle) have mouthpieces assembled from seven individual parts, all fabricated from sheet (Tarr, *The Trumpet*, 51). A seventeenth-century mouthpiece in the Carl Claudius' Collection in Copenhagen has a sheet-metal shank soldered to a cast cup. There appears to have been little or no taper on the shanks of these early mouthpieces, and it is only with the advent of one-piece castings that a 'standard' taper evolved.

7

Conclusion

I make trumpets with two holes: a small one at one end, into which one blows, and a large one at the other end, out of which the sound comes.

R. Barclay (attrib.)

Now that we have followed a reasonably detailed description of how a trumpet-maker of several centuries ago might have constructed and finished an instrument, we are left with the general question 'why'? Why should the systematic analysis of early technique be of value to the instrument-maker and player of today? Why should this information be of more than simply academic interest?

By illustrating the previous chapter with photographs and drawings of processes recreated in a twentieth-century workshop, there is the quite obvious intention of demonstrating the practical possibility of constructing instruments in a thoroughly authentic fashion. But if this were all this book had set out to achieve, it would conclude half fulfilled. Indeed, Chapter 6, and the preceding chapters which lay the groundwork, do not simply propose an alternative way of making early trumpets—they outline the proper and correct way of doing the job. Making trumpets the original way is proper and correct for three basic reasons: it is philosophically sound, it is ethically sound, and it leads to more responsive instruments. These three aspects are examined in the following sections.

The High Philosophical Road

Philosphical soundness merely requires the player to use the correct equipment because that is the way it was done originally. It is a very simple concept, approachable by only a few. It is right that each player knows his or her limitations, but the line must clearly be drawn when inauthentic equipment is used in supposedly authentic performance. There is no shame in falling short of some abstract and entirely flexible ideal, provided it is done with integrity and honesty. But authentic performance demands consistency. There is little point in delving deeply into style and articulation if one's instrumentation differs significantly from that used when the music was new.

When arguing for handmade versus machine-made, or natural versus compromised, one is arguing for a degree of imperfection. It would be satisfying to believe that the visual and technical imperfection of a handmade instrument had a parallel in the musical imperfection of the natural harmonic series. Therefore, if a maker was permitted to leave the marks of his tools on the surface for all to see, could not the player leave the marks of his efforts in less than perfect tuning of the odd harmonic? Perhaps in these days players (or their directors) cannot allow themselves this liberty, knowing that every glitch and imperfection can be scrutinized over and over again by a mass record-buying public. Perhaps, also, the instrument-makers among the readership of this book no longer dare to make retrograde steps for fear of losing their markets. Even the finest hand-work is not flawless, and can be disparaged by those accustomed to machine-made perfection. This author has been criticized for the statement that no two of his instruments are the same; a statement of which he remains proud. Hand-work must not be flawless because it must reflect the mind and hands of its creator. The same is true for music.

Ultimately, the craftsman who decides, for whatever reason, to re-create an instrument as closely as possible to a historic model has made a deep commitment. He is justified in expecting an equivalent commitment from the user of his products.

The Ethical High Ground

Ideally, early music should always be played upon original instruments of the correct period and provenance. Record liner notes lead us to believe this is a fairly widespread practice, at least among the strings; the wind instruments are not so well represented, and in view of what follows, this is no bad thing. All else being equal (although it never is) use of correct original instruments would allow players to concentrate on the musical aspects of the work, rather than the mere tools. There are several good reasons why this is only occasionally possible; apart from the availability of suitable original instruments, well made, in good condition, and at reasonable prices, ethical considerations in bringing early instruments to a working state play an important part. Discussions on care of musical instruments in both public and private collections have centred around the problems of restoration versus conservation and it has become evident that restoration of instruments has resulted in many cases of irreversible damage to unique examples and significant loss of historical evidence. Although a clear distinction exists between the practices of private owners and restorers of musical instruments and those expected of personnel working in and for museum collections, the compromises to the integrity of the instruments in both domains remain an unfortunate constant. The ethical dilemma revolves around the definition and application of the terms 'conservation' and 'restoration'. *The Code of Ethics and Guidance for Practice*[1] defines conservation, in part, as:

All actions aimed at the safeguarding of cultural property for the future. The purpose of conservation is to study, record, retain and restore the culturally significant qualities of the object with the least possible intervention (p. 18).

The chief aim of conservation treatment is stabilization in a present state. If an instrument is unplayable, pure conservation treatment will not make it otherwise. In the specific case of brass instruments, the 'least possible intervention' might preclude such treatments as polishing, soldering, straightening and dent removal. It could be argued on ethical grounds that all the above operations might remove or compromise information of cultural value. Restoration, on the other hand, is defined in the same document as follows:

All actions taken to modify the existing materials and structure of a cultural property to represent a known earlier state. The aim of restoration is to preserve and reveal the aesthetic and historical value of a cultural property. Restoration is based on respect for the remaining original material and clear evidence of an earlier state. (p. 19)

On the surface, restoration has always appeared a desirable end. Metal is such a tractable material that repairs and alterations are more likely than not to be found on early instruments. However, reshaping, soldering, and polishing, three of the chief techniques available to the brass-instrument-restorer, are detrimental to the physical integrity of the object to which they are applied, no matter how much respect one may show for it. It is therefore difficult, if not impossible, to perform a full restoration without compromise; without, in fact, contravening the museum-based codes of ethics for conservation.

More subtle and less obvious are the acoustic considerations accompanying restoration to a presupposed original condition. We know of the ageing properties of brass. Players attest that there is a difference between the resonance of an old instrument and that of a faithful modern copy, but did the old instrument resonate the way it does now when it left the maker's workshop? Does the natural ageing of brass, the growth of intergranular microfissures, affect the acoustics in a perceptible way? It is also known that machine-made tubing responds very differently from handmade material. What acoustic effects will result from reworking old material and adding new pieces? In the end we cannot know if our painstakingly restored

---

[1] These definitions are taken from the *Code of Ethics* produced by the International Institute for Conservation—Canadian Group (see Bibliography) which has produced the most thoughtful and cogent document to date. It should be borne in mind, though, that codes of ethics, especially in the museum field, cannot dictate courses of action; they can only guide.

original instrument is doing quite what its maker intended. We can approach an understanding, but it will always elude us in the end. This fact alone should caution us to do little rather than much.

It can be convincingly argued that a faithful copy of an early brass instrument can perform more 'authentically' than an original restored to what approximates a supposed primary state. The oft-heard criticism that reproductions never come close enough for scholarly purposes is a prime example of vague and woolly thinking. It remains to be seen how close it is possible to come, or even necessary to come, in order to satisfy academic requirements, should there ever be a way of defining them. The ethical high ground, which suppports the systematic making of reproductions, as opposed to restoration of originals, is not by any means a difficult course to take in satisfying the practical requirements of musicians while still fulfilling the needs of authenticity.

Better Response

If the knowledge of a job well done were the only reward that the maker of authentic instruments and the conscientious player could enjoy, the practice would be limited to a very few. Not many nowadays can take reward from virtue alone. Few working trumpet players can afford to take the high philosophical road or the ethical high ground to performance practice; in today's competitive music market they would soon starve. So would makers who took the time and trouble to work in an entirely authentic fashion, if they only knew how. On the other hand, if there were a tangible practical reason why playing an authentically made instrument might be more desirable, even those long accustomed to making compromises might be willing to experiment.

Not many players of today have worked consistently with good museum instruments or faithfully handmade copies. In this author's experience the playing quality of handmade instruments is far superior to equivalent machine-made ones. One case among many will illustrate this point: some years ago a copy of an instrument by Johann Carl Kodisch was equipped with modern extruded brass tubing and delivered to the client. Later, when the techniques for producing rolled and seamed tubing were better mastered, the client requested that this instrument be retubed with the proper material. Once this was done the playing quality improved profoundly. Nothing had been altered in dimensions or material—simply, the tubing was less smooth and less consistent. The client found that it was easier to 'bend' the out-of-tune harmonics by 'lipping them in' without them breaking to the next in sequence. It appeared that the latitude for pitch adjustment was wider. Acoustic tests have lent support to this contention: 'in spite of the perfection of modern, machine-made components as opposed to the irregularities in eighteenth century handmade construction, the old instruments are much easier to play and are more in tune than modern facsimiles' (Smithers, *et al.*, 115). The response of an instrument is determined by the so-called Q factor of the resonance, and this is related (inter alia) to the smoothness and consistency of the inner walls of the tubing. Not only is handmade tubing inconsistent, but the jointed construction of the yards, bows, and bellpipe ensures a lower Q factor and consequent easier manipulation of the harmonics. However, this observation is based primarily upon the author's experience and will probably remain a rather simplistic generalization until more studies on original instruments and modern copies are carried out. For example, certain instruments made using alternative techniques actually have excellent intonation and are beautifully playable.[2] There is a mystery here which at the present escapes elucidation. Whatever the case, insufficient acoustic evidence exists to do anything but generalize.

Following are some of the many factors which have been said, knowingly or otherwise, to contribute in some way to tone formation and playability of brass instruments: thin versus thick metal for the bell; handmade versus machine-made tubing; bell and bow shape; method of assembly of components; quantities of constituents and purity of alloys; hammering of the bell versus spinning; the diameter of the tubing; and lead versus other alloys for bending. The literature unfortunately abounds with half-truths, assertions, misinterpretations, and just plain nonsense. Much work has already been done to clear away some of this fog by exploring and defining acoustical parameters,[3] but whether this work can be efficiently disseminated to those who would most benefit is a moot point.

If the high philosophical road for its own sake is seen as leading only to penury and dissatisfaction, it may be that the tangibly superior playing qualities of the real thing will convince players to put aside their present collections of plumbing and make a few simple experiments. It might also convince trumpet-makers that there may, indeed, be a profit in doing things this way, and that authentic practice might not be confined solely to amateurs of independent means. Naturally, instruments laboriously produced by hand cost more than equivalent ones made quickly on ma-

---

[2] David Edwards' copies of English instruments by Simon Beale and John Harris are superb evidence of this. He believes that his copies work so well because they exactly follow the dimensions of the originals; i.e. the ratio of the length of the bell flare to the length of the parallel tubing, and the exact flare of the bell. The profile of the bell is highly significant; his early trial-and-error attempts (before obtaining permission to copy the Harris and Beale instruments) led to incorrect harmonics being produced.

[3] As well as the excellent work of Smithers, Wogram, and Bowsher (which is still in progress) the acoustic work of A. H. Benade and his colleagues is of particular interest to the modern study of tone formation in brass instruments. Also, in a series of experiments using a variety of bell profiles, J. C. Webster of the C. G. Conn Company showed that bell shape was a critical factor in the tuning of the instrument's harmonics. He also showed the extent to which a skilled player can compensate for the idiosyncracies of his instrument (see Bibliography).

chines, but this has always been the case in the musical-instrument industry and has been a stimulus, not a deterrent, to determined artists and craftsmen in both wood and metal.

Final Words

It is very easy to speak of 'exact copies' but this is naturally an ideal which is only approachable and never attainable. The effort expended on attempting to approach this ideal will never be repaid, because our aim is not slavish re-creation; our aim is the creative interpretation of the original work based upon sound evidence of early practice. This is so with music, and it is equally so with instrument-making. And this process, whether it be in the making of instruments or the making of music on them, can never get off the ground without good tools and the wherewithal to use them faithfully.

   It is pointless to attempt close copying of selected trumpets until their worth as musical instruments has been established beyond dispute. This is especially true of trumpets in museum collections, the majority of which were only spared trampling under hooves on the field of battle by happenstance of history. Many of these museum pieces are of dubious craftsmanship and quite probably not good musical instruments.[4] This is not, however, a hard and fast rule; the finest craftsmanship was often reserved for gorgeous ceremonial instruments whose musical qualities might never have been truly tested. On the other hand, there is nothing to preclude field instruments of crude manufacture being, coincidentally, good performers. But this does raise the question of which surviving early instruments are best to copy, and how their value should be judged. While one would hardly wish to advocate the wholesale opening of museum collections for acoustic experiments, there is clearly a need for skilled players to assess from the many extant instruments in original condition the best instruments for copying,[5] though it should be remembered that a player used to using pitch correcting contraptions of whatever kind may not be the best judge of the playing qualities of a natural instrument.

   [4] The prices of Nuremberg trumpets and trombones on the international market are shocking, especially when one compares their workmanship with that of beautifully made and embellished presentation bugles of the 19th cent. which can be acquired for a tenth the price. Mere workmanship apparently has no influence on value.

   [5] There has been much controversy in the musical instrument museum world over public access to museum collections, and damage which has resulted to some items during examination and measurement. This has prompted the production of a small booklet by the Comité international des musées et collections d'instruments de musique (CIMCIM) of the International Council of Museums. Most musical instrument museums possess a copy of *Recommendations for Regulating the Access to Musical Instruments in Public Collections* and abide by its guidelines (see Bibliography).

Reasonably accurate copies of natural trumpets from museum collections have been available from manufacturers for decades, but there is certainly little evidence of their consistent use in uncompromised form in the Baroque orchestra to date. It therefore remains to be proven that the models chosen for these copies were actually the best for the intended purpose. An original which played well in *principale*, for example, may not have been good in the *clarino* register, and vice versa. Also, the playability of the copies might well have been compromised by techniques of mass manufacture. The evidence resulting from the widespread lack of use of factory copies in a natural form certainly indicates problems beyond simply the competence of players. Perhaps before this decade has passed the whole controversy of the playability of the instrument and the willingness of the player will have been reassessed and the trumpet will finally take its place among all the other instruments of the Baroque orchestra whose teething problems are far in the past.

BIBLIOGRAPHY AND FURTHER READING

AGRICOLA, G., *De Natura Fossilium* (1546), trans. M. C. Bandy and J. A. Bandy (The Geological Society of America, Special Paper 63, 1955).

—— *De Re Metallica* (1556), trans. H. C. Hoover and L. H. Hoover, (New York: Dover, 1950).

ALTENBURG, D., *Untersuchung zur Geschichte der Trompete in Zeitalter der Clarinblaskunst* (Regensburg: Gustav Bose Verlag, 1973).

ALTENBURG, J. E., *Versuch einer Anleitung zur heroisch-musikalischen Trompeter- und Pauker-Kunst* (Halle, 1795), trans. E. H. Tarr, (Nashville: The Brass Press, 1974).

(American Society for Metals, *Metals Handbook*, viii: *Metallography, Structures and Phase Diagrams* (Cleveland, Ohio: American Society for Metals, 1973).

AMMAN, J., and SACHS, H., *Ständebuch* (1568); facsimile reproduction as *Book of Trades*, with introduction by B. Rifkin (New York: Dover, 1973).

Anonymous, *The Boy's Book of Trades and Tools Used in Them* (London: George Routledge & Sons, c.1850).

Anonymous, *Mappae Clavicula*, trans. C. S. Smith and J. G. Hawthorne, *Transactions of the American Philosophical Society*, 64: 4, (1974).

BAINES, A., *Brass Instruments* (London: Faber and Faber, 1976).

—— 'James Talbot's Manuscript (Christ Church Library, Music MS 1187) I. Wind Instruments', *Galpin Society Journal*, 1 (1948).

BALL, J. N., *Merchants and Merchandise* (London: Croom Helm, 1977).

BARCLAY, R., *The Care of Musical Instruments in Canadian Collections*, Technical Bulletin No. 4, rev. edn. (Ottawa: Canadian Conservation Institute, 1982).

—— 'Ethics in the Conservation and Restoration of Early Brass Instruments', *Historic Brass Society Journal*, 1: 1 (1989), 75–81.

—— 'Preliminary Studies on Trumpet Making Techniques in 17th and 18th Century Nürnberg', *Festschrift für John Henry van der Meer zu seinem fünfundsechzigsten Geburtstag* (Tutzig: H. Schneider, 1987).

BARRACLOUGH, K. C., *Sheffield Steel* (Buxton: Moorland Publishing Company, 1976).

BATE, P., *The Trumpet and Trombone* (London: Ernest Benn, 1978).

BEDINI, S. A., and PRICE, D. J. de S., 'Instrumentation', in M. Kranzberg and C. W. Pursell Jr. (eds.), *Technology in Western Civilization*, i (New York: Oxford University Press, 1967).

BENADE, A. H., 'The Physics of Brasses', *The Physics of Music* (readings from *Scientific American*), (San Francisco: W. H. Freeman and Co., 1978), 44–55.

—— 'The Physics of Wood Winds', *The Physics of Music* (readings from *Scientific American*), (San Francisco: W. H. Freeman and Co., 1978), 35–43.

BERNER, A., VAN DER MEER, J. H., and THIBAULT, G., *Preservation and Restoration of Musical Instruments* (Paris: International Council of Museums, 1967).

BIRINGUCCIO, V., *Pirotechnia* (1540), trans. C. S. Smith (Boston: MIT Press, 1966).

BUTTS, A., and COX, C. D. (eds.), *Silver: Economics, Metallurgy, and Use* (Huntingdon, NY: Robert E. Kreiger, 1975).

CARSE, A., *Musical Wind Instruments* (New York: Da Capo Press, 1965).

CARTER, G. F., *Principles of Physical and Chemical Metallurgy* (Cleveland, Ohio: American Society for Metals, 1979).

CELLINI, B., *Treatise on Goldsmithing* (1568), trans. C. R. Ashbee (New York: Dover, 1967).

CLOSSON, E., *Le Facteur des instruments de musique en Belgique* (Brussels, 1935).

Comité international des musées et collections d'instruments de musique, *Recommendations for Regulating the Access to Musical Instruments in Public Collections* (Paris: Comité international des musées et collections d'instruments de musique (CIMCIM), 1983).

CRADDOCK, P. T., 'The Compositions of the Copper Alloys Used by the Greek, Etruscan and Roman Civilizations. 3. The Origins and Early Use of Brass', *Journal of Archaeological Science*, 5: 1 (1978), 1–16.

CROSSLEY, D. W. (ed.), *Medieval Industry*, Research Report No. 40 (London: Council for British Archaeology, 1981).

DAWKINS, J. M., *Zinc and Spelter* (Oxford: Zinc Development Association, 1950).

DICK, W. B., *Dick's Encyclopedia of Practical Receipts and Processes* (1870) (facsimile reproduction, New York: Funk and Wagnall's, n.d.).

DIDEROT, D., and D'ALEMBERT, J. LE R., *Encyclopédie* (Paris, 1751–72) (facsimile reproduction, Paris: H. Veyrier, 1965).

DOWNEY, P., 'The Renaissance Slide Trumpet', *Early Music*, 12: 1 (1984), 26–33.

ERCKER, L., *Beschreibung allefürnemsten mineralischen Ertzt- und Bergwercksarten* (1580), *Treatise on Ores and Assaying*, (1580) trans. A. G. Sisco and C. S. Smith (Chicago: University of Chicago Press, 1951).

FISCHER, H. G., *The Renaissance Sackbut and Its Use Today* (New York: Metropolitan Museum of Art, 1984).

—— 'The Tenor Sackbut of Anton Schnitzer the Elder at Nice', *Historic Brass Society Journal*, 1 (1989), 65–74.

FLICK, J. J., *Vollständige theoretische und praktische Geschichte der Erfindungen* (Basel, 1798).

GALON, *L'Art de convertir le cuivre rouge, ou cuivre en rosette, en laiton, ou cuivre jaune* (Paris, 1764).

GORDON, R. B., 'Metallography of Brass in a 16th Century Astrolabe', *Journal of the Historical Metallurgy Society*, 20: 2 (1986), 93–6.

GUG, R., 'Historical and Experimental Studies on Brass Used for Reed Tongues', *International Society of Organists*, 28 (1988), 27–58.

HACHENBERG, K., 'Der Werkstoffe Messing im mitteleuropäischen Instrumentenbau vom 16. bis Ende des 18. Jahrhunderts', *Instrumentenbau*, 44: 9 (Sept. 1988).

HAEDEKE, H.-U., *Metalwork* (Universe Books, New York, 1970).

HALLE, J. S., *Werkstäte der heutigen Künste*, iii (Brandenburg: J. W. and J. S. Halle, 1764).

HASKELL, H., *The Early Music Revival* (London: Thames and Hudson, 1988).

HASSE, M. T., *Vorzüglichsten Künste und mit Kunst verbundenen Handweke . . . zum Gebrauch für Schulen* (Königsberg, 1792).

HELLWIG, F., 'Conservation and Restoration', in C. Ford (ed.), *Making Musical Instruments* (London: Faber and Faber, 1979).

HEYDE, H., *Musikinstrumentenbau: 15.–19. Jahrhundert Kunst-Handwerk Entwurf* (Wiesbaden: Breitkopf & Härtel, 1986).

—— *Trompeten, posaunen, Tuben* (Wiesbaden: Breitkopf und Härtel, 1985).

HODGES, H., *Artifacts* (London: John Baker, 1976).

HULL, D. R., *Casting of Brass and Bronze: Some Practical Aspects of Casting Brass and Bronze in America, 1900 to 1950* (Cleveland, Ohio: American Society for Metals, 1950).

IGARUSHI, J., and KOYASU, M., 'Acoustical Properties of Trumpets', *Journal of the Acoustical Society of America*, 25 (1953), 122–8.

International Institute for Conservation—Canadian Group and Canadian Association of Professional Art Conservators, *Code of Ethics and Guidance for Practice*, 2nd edn. (Ottawa: International Institute for Conservation—Canadian Group and Canadian Association of Professional Art Conservators, 1989).

International Council of Museums, *ICOM Statutes/Code of Professional Ethics* (Paris: International Council of Museums, 1987).

KARP, C., 'Musical Instruments Recovered from the Royal Swedish Flagship *Kronan* (1676)', *Second Conference of the ICTM Study Group on Music Archaeology*, Royal Swedish Acadamy of Music, Stockholm, 1 (1986), 95–104.

—— 'Restoration, Conservation, Repair and Maintenance', *Early Music*, 7: 1 (1979), 79–84.

—— 'Technological Research and the Conservation of Musical Instruments', in L. S. Olschki (ed.), *Per Una Carta Europea del Restauro* (Florence: Società Italiana di Musicologia, 1987), 283–9.

KLEIN, J. G. F., *Beschreibung der Metall-Lothe und Löthungen* (Berlin, 1760).

KRÜGER, W., 'Metallblasinstrumente, ihre physikalische Wirkungsweise und die Wechselwirkung zwischen Konstruktion und akustischem Verhalten', *Konservierung und Restaurierung, Nachbau und auffürungspraktische Nutzung von Metallblasinstrumenten* (Berlin: Nationaler Museumsrat der DDR, 1985.)

KRÜNITZ, J. G., *Ökonomisch-technologische Encyklopädie* (Berlin, 1802).

LANGWILL, L. G., *Index of Musical Wind Instrument Makers* (5th edn., Edinburgh: Lindsay and Co., 1972).

LIETZMANN, K.-D., SCHLEGEL, J., and HENSEL, A., *Metall-Formung* (Leipzig:VEB Deutscher Verlag für Grundstoffindustrie, 1983).

LOCKNER, H. P., *Messing: 15.–17. Jahrhundert* (Munich: Klinkhardt & Biermann, 1982).

McDONALD, A. S., PRICE, B. R., and SISTARE, G. H., 'Alloying Behaviour of Silver and its Principle Binary Alloys', in A. Butts (ed.), *Silver: Economics, Metallurgy and Use* (Huntingdon, NY: Robert E. Kreiger), 1975, 235–71.

McDONALD, D., 'The History of Silver', in A. Butts (ed.), *Silver: Economics, Metallurgy and Use*, (Huntingdon, NY: Robert E. Kreiger, 1975), 1–15.

MARYON, H., *Metalwork and Enamelling* (New York: Dover, 1971).

MEEK, J. B., *The Art of Engraving* (Montezuma, Ia.: F. Brownell and Son, 1973).

MENZEL, U., 'Die Antwendung traditioneller Techniken bei der Restaurierung historischer Blechblasinstrumente', *Musical Instrument Conservation and Technology Journal (MICAT)*, 1 (1978), 31–42.

—— 'Über traditionalle Handwerkstechniken bei der Herstelling von Blechblasinstrumenten', *Newsletter of Comité international des musées et collections d'instruments de musique (CIMCIM)*, 13 (1988), 42–9.

MITCHINER, M. B., MORTIMER, C., and POLLARD, A. M., 'Nuremberg and its Jetons', *Numismatic Chronicle*, 147 (1987), 114–55.

MOECK, H. (ed.) *Fünf Jahrhunderte deutscher Musikinstrumentenbau* (Celle: Moeck Verlag, 1987).

MORTON, C., *Transactions of the Royal Society*, 51: 2, (London, 1760), 936.

MOXON, J., *Mechanick Exercises or the Doctrine of Handy-Works* (London, 1703) (repr., Scarsdale, NY: The Early American Industries Association, 1979).

NÖDL, K., *Metalblasinstrumentenbau* (Frankfurt-on-Main: Verlag des Musikinstrumenten, 1970).

PANOFSKY, E., *Meaning in the Visual Arts* (Garden City, NY: Doubleday Anchor, 1955).

PERESS, M., 'A Baroque Trumpet Discovered in Greenwich Village', *Brass Quarterly*, 4: 3 (1961), 121.

PLENDERLEITH, H. J., and WERNER, A. E. A., *The Conservation of Antiquities and Works of Art* (London: Oxford University Press, 1971).

PLINY, *Naturalis Historiae*, Book 34.2, trans. H. Rackham (London: Heinemann, 1968).

PRAETORIUS, M., *Syntagma Musicum* (Wolfenbüttel, 1619) (facsimile reproduction, Kassel, 1958).

RABINOWICZ, E., 'Polishing', *Scientific American*, 218: 6 (1986), 91–9.

RAUB, Ch. J., 'The Development of Gilding from Antiquity to the Middle Ages', *Materials Australasia*, 18:9 (1986), 7–11.

ROGERS, B. A., *The Nature of Metals* (Cambridge, Mass.: The MIT Press, 1964).

SCHOPPER, H., *De omnibus illiberalibus sive mechanicis artibus humani generis*, illustrated by Jost Amman (Frankfurt-on-Main, 1574).

SMITH, C. S., and FORBES, R. J., 'Metallurgy and Assaying', *A History of Technology*, iii, ed. S. Singer, E. J. Holmyard, A. R. Mall, and T. I. Williams (Oxford: Oxford University Press, 1957).

SMITHERS, D. L., *The Music and History of the Baroque Trumpet Before 1721*, 2nd edn.) (Carbondale, Ill.: Southern Illinois University Press, 1988).

—— 'The Trumpets of J. W. Haas: A Survey of Four Generations of Nuremberg Brass Instrument Makers', *Galpin Society Journal*, 18 (1965), 23–41.

—— WOGRAM, K., and BOWSHER, J., 'Playing the Baroque Trumpet', *Scientific American*, 254: 4 (1986), 108–15.

STRAUSS, G., *Nuremberg in the Sixteenth Century* (New York: John Wiley & Sons, 1966).

Symposium for Restorers of Non-Keyboard Instruments, Germanisches Nationalmuseum (Nuremberg, 1974), 'Discussion', *Musical Instrument Conservation and Technology*, 1 (1978), 39–42.

TARR, E., 'Cesare Bendinelli (ca. 1542–1617)', *Brass Bulletin*, 17 (1977), 31–45, and 21 (1978), 13–25.

—— *The Trumpet* (London: B. T. Batsford, 1988).

—— and Buser, E. W., *Die Trompete: Instrumente und Dokumente vom Barock bis zur Gegenwart* (Bad Säckingen: Trompeterschloss Bad Säckingen, n.d.)

THEIN, H., and THEIN, M., 'Bericht über die Untersuchung und Restaurierung der Haas-Trompete, Inventarnummer Ea 14–1942, des Gemeentemuseums Den Haag', unpublished report (Bremen, n.d.).

—— and —— 'Zur Geschichte der Renaissance-Posaune von Jörg Neuschel (1557) und ihrer Nachschöpfung', *Basler Jahrbuch für historische Musikpraxis*, 5 (1981), 377–404.

THEOPHILUS, *De Diversis Artibus*, trans. as *On Divers Arts*, J. G. Hawthorne and C. S. Smith (Chicago: University of Chicago Press, 1963).

TYLECOTE, R. F., *The Early History of Metallurgy in Europe* (London: Longman, 1987).

—— *A History of Metallurgy* (London: The Metals Society, 1976).

UHLIG, H. H. (ed.), *The Corrosion Handbook* (New York: The Electrochemical Society, John Wiley & Sons, 1948).

ULLWER, H., 'Die Eigenschaften von Messingblech in Abhängigkeit von der Herstellungsbedingungen', *Konservierung und Restaurierung, Nachbau und auffürungspraktische Nutzung von Metallblasinstrumenten* (Berlin: Nationaler Museumsrat der DDR, 1985.)

UNTRACT, O., *Metal Techniques for Craftsmen* (Garden City, NY: Doubleday, 1975).

VAN DER MEER, J. H., *Verzeichnis der Europäischen Musikinstrumente im Germanisches Nationalmuseum Nürnberg*, i (Nuremberg: Germanisches Nationalmuseum, 1979).

WEBER, R., 'Lote und Flußmittel in Quellen des 17. und 18. Jahrhunderts', *Konservierung und Restaurierung, Nachbau und auffürungspraktische Nutzung von Metallblasinstrumenten* (Berlin: Nationaler Museumsrat der DDR, 1985.)

WEBSTER, J., 'Internal Tuning Differences due to Players and the Taper of Trumpet Bells', *Journal of the Acoustical Society of America*, 21: 3 (1949), 208–14.

WEIGEL, C., *Abbildung der gemein nützlichen Hauptstände* (Regensburg, 1698).

WÖRTHMÜLLER, W., 'Die Instrumente der Nürnberger Trompeten- und Posaunenmacher', *Mittelungen des Vereins für Geschichte des Stadt Nürnberg*, 46 (1955), 372–478.

—— 'Die Nürnberger Trompeten- und Posaunenmacher des 17. und 18. jahrhunderts', *Mittelungen des Vereins für Geschichte des Stadt Nürnberg*, 45 (1954), 209–325.

YAPP, P., *The Traveller's Dictionary of Quotation* (London: Routledge & Kegan Paul, 1983).

INDEX